Division Speed & Accuracy Log

Practice

	Time	0'00"	1'00"	2'00"	3'00"	4'00"	5'00" Score
13	′ ″						
14	′ ″						
15	′ ″						
16	′ ″						
17	′ ″						
18	′ ″						
19	′ ″						
20	′ ″						
21	′ ″						
22	′ ″						
23	′ ″						
24	′ ″						
25	′ ″						
26	′ ″						
27	′ ″						
28	′ ″						
29	′ ″						
30	′ ″						
31	′ ″						
32	′ ″						
33	′ ″						
34	′ ″						
35	′ ″						
36	′ ″						
37	′ ″						
38	′ ″						
39	′ ″						
40	′ ″						

Sprint

	Time	0'00"	1'00"	2'00"	3'00"	4'00"	5'00" Score
41	′ ″						
42	′ ″						
43	′ ″						
44	′ ″						
45	′ ″						
46	′ ″						
47	′ ″						
48	′ ″						
49	′ ″						
50	′ ″						
51	′ ″						
52	′ ″						
53	′ ″						
54	′ ″						
55	′ ″						
56	′ ″						

How to log your results

Write your time and score for each page. Plot your results in the graph with a dot and connect the dots to show your progress.

Example		Time	0'00"	1'00"	2'00"	3'00"	4'00"	5'00" Score
	13	2' 30"						45
	14	3' 30"						38
	15	2' 33"						43
	16	2' 40"						40
	17	3' 00"						37
	18	2' 30"						45
	19	2' 10"						

As you work through the book, your progress may vary, but your speed and accuracy will surely improve. Continue to log your time and score to see the positive changes—you may get faster, become more accurate, and/or feel more confident in your skills. Pay close attention to any changes you observe.

Date / / **Name**

1 **Read each number sentence aloud. Trace each answer.**

① $2 \div 2 = 1$ ④ $8 \div 2 = 4$ ⑦ $14 \div 2 = 7$

② $4 \div 2 = 2$ ⑤ $10 \div 2 = 5$ ⑧ $16 \div 2 = 8$

③ $6 \div 2 = 3$ ⑥ $12 \div 2 = 6$ ⑨ $18 \div 2 = 9$

2 **Divide. Time how long it takes to complete the division problems. Log your time below.**

① $2 \div 2 =$ ⑪ $6 \div 2 =$ ㉑ $18 \div 2 =$

② $4 \div 2 =$ ⑫ $10 \div 2 =$ ㉒ $6 \div 2 =$

③ $6 \div 2 =$ ⑬ $14 \div 2 =$ ㉓ $12 \div 2 =$

④ $8 \div 2 =$ ⑭ $18 \div 2 =$ ㉔ $16 \div 2 =$

⑤ $10 \div 2 =$ ⑮ $4 \div 2 =$ ㉕ $10 \div 2 =$

⑥ $12 \div 2 =$ ⑯ $8 \div 2 =$ ㉖ $4 \div 2 =$

⑦ $14 \div 2 =$ ⑰ $12 \div 2 =$ ㉗ $18 \div 2 =$

⑧ $16 \div 2 =$ ⑱ $16 \div 2 =$ ㉘ $2 \div 2 =$

⑨ $18 \div 2 =$ ⑲ $10 \div 2 =$ ㉙ $14 \div 2 =$

⑩ $2 \div 2 =$ ⑳ $14 \div 2 =$ ㉚ $8 \div 2 =$

Review any incorrect answers and remember not to rush.

Score

Your Time

min.   sec.   /39

2 Warm-Up Division ÷3

Date / /   Name

1 Read each number sentence aloud. Trace each answer.

① 3 ÷ 3 = 1   ④ 12 ÷ 3 = 4   ⑦ 21 ÷ 3 = 7

② 6 ÷ 3 = 2   ⑤ 15 ÷ 3 = 5   ⑧ 24 ÷ 3 = 8

③ 9 ÷ 3 = 3   ⑥ 18 ÷ 3 = 6   ⑨ 27 ÷ 3 = 9

2 Divide. Time how long it takes to complete the division problems. Log your time below.

① 3 ÷ 3 =   ⑪ 12 ÷ 3 =   ㉑ 21 ÷ 3 =

② 6 ÷ 3 =   ⑫ 18 ÷ 3 =   ㉒ 3 ÷ 3 =

③ 9 ÷ 3 =   ⑬ 24 ÷ 3 =   ㉓ 24 ÷ 3 =

④ 12 ÷ 3 =   ⑭ 3 ÷ 3 =   ㉔ 18 ÷ 3 =

⑤ 15 ÷ 3 =   ⑮ 9 ÷ 3 =   ㉕ 12 ÷ 3 =

⑥ 18 ÷ 3 =   ⑯ 15 ÷ 3 =   ㉖ 27 ÷ 3 =

⑦ 21 ÷ 3 =   ⑰ 21 ÷ 3 =   ㉗ 6 ÷ 3 =

⑧ 24 ÷ 3 =   ⑱ 27 ÷ 3 =   ㉘ 15 ÷ 3 =

⑨ 27 ÷ 3 =   ⑲ 6 ÷ 3 =   ㉙ 9 ÷ 3 =

⑩ 6 ÷ 3 =   ⑳ 9 ÷ 3 =   ㉚ 24 ÷ 3 =

Your Time   min.   sec.

Score   /39

Warm-Up
Division ÷4

Date / /   **Name**

1 **Read each number sentence aloud. Trace each answer.**

① $4 \div 4 = 1$ ④ $16 \div 4 = 4$ ⑦ $28 \div 4 = 7$

② $8 \div 4 = 2$ ⑤ $20 \div 4 = 5$ ⑧ $32 \div 4 = 8$

③ $12 \div 4 = 3$ ⑥ $24 \div 4 = 6$ ⑨ $36 \div 4 = 9$

2 **Divide. Time how long it takes to complete the division problems. Log your time below.**

① $4 \div 4 =$ ⑪ $12 \div 4 =$ ㉑ $8 \div 4 =$

② $8 \div 4 =$ ⑫ $20 \div 4 =$ ㉒ $16 \div 4 =$

③ $12 \div 4 =$ ⑬ $28 \div 4 =$ ㉓ $24 \div 4 =$

④ $16 \div 4 =$ ⑭ $36 \div 4 =$ ㉔ $32 \div 4 =$

⑤ $20 \div 4 =$ ⑮ $8 \div 4 =$ ㉕ $36 \div 4 =$

⑥ $24 \div 4 =$ ⑯ $16 \div 4 =$ ㉖ $12 \div 4 =$

⑦ $28 \div 4 =$ ⑰ $24 \div 4 =$ ㉗ $28 \div 4 =$

⑧ $32 \div 4 =$ ⑱ $32 \div 4 =$ ㉘ $4 \div 4 =$

⑨ $36 \div 4 =$ ⑲ $4 \div 4 =$ ㉙ $24 \div 4 =$

⑩ $4 \div 4 =$ ⑳ $20 \div 4 =$ ㉚ $16 \div 4 =$

Your Time

min.   sec.

Score

/39

4

Warm-Up

Review: Division from ÷2 to ÷4

Date / / Name

● **Divide. Time how long it takes to complete the division problems. Log your time below.**

① 2 ÷ 2 =

② 4 ÷ 2 =

③ 6 ÷ 2 =

④ 8 ÷ 2 =

⑤ 10 ÷ 2 =

⑥ 12 ÷ 2 =

⑦ 14 ÷ 2 =

⑧ 16 ÷ 2 =

⑨ 18 ÷ 2 =

⑩ 3 ÷ 3 =

⑪ 6 ÷ 3 =

⑫ 9 ÷ 3 =

⑬ 12 ÷ 3 =

⑭ 15 ÷ 3 =

⑮ 18 ÷ 3 =

⑯ 21 ÷ 3 =

⑰ 24 ÷ 3 =

⑱ 27 ÷ 3 =

⑲ 4 ÷ 4 =

⑳ 8 ÷ 4 =

㉑ 12 ÷ 4 =

㉒ 16 ÷ 4 =

㉓ 20 ÷ 4 =

㉔ 24 ÷ 4 =

㉕ 28 ÷ 4 =

㉖ 32 ÷ 4 =

㉗ 36 ÷ 4 =

㉘ 14 ÷ 2 =

㉙ 6 ÷ 3 =

㉚ 36 ÷ 4 =

㉛ 2 ÷ 2 =

㉜ 9 ÷ 3 =

㉝ 16 ÷ 4 =

㉞ 18 ÷ 2 =

㉟ 3 ÷ 3 =

㊱ 20 ÷ 4 =

㊲ 6 ÷ 2 =

㊳ 24 ÷ 3 =

㊴ 8 ÷ 4 =

㊵ 8 ÷ 2 =

㊶ 21 ÷ 3 =

㊷ 4 ÷ 4 =

㊸ 16 ÷ 2 =

㊹ 15 ÷ 3 =

㊺ 24 ÷ 4 =

Your Time min. sec.

Score /45

1 **Read each number sentence aloud. Trace each answer.**

① $5 \div 5 = 1$ ④ $20 \div 5 = 4$ ⑦ $35 \div 5 = 7$

② $10 \div 5 = 2$ ⑤ $25 \div 5 = 5$ ⑧ $40 \div 5 = 8$

③ $15 \div 5 = 3$ ⑥ $30 \div 5 = 6$ ⑨ $45 \div 5 = 9$

2 **Divide. Time how long it takes to complete the division problems. Log your time below.**

① $5 \div 5 =$ ⑪ $20 \div 5 =$ ㉑ $5 \div 5 =$

② $10 \div 5 =$ ⑫ $30 \div 5 =$ ㉒ $40 \div 5 =$

③ $15 \div 5 =$ ⑬ $40 \div 5 =$ ㉓ $20 \div 5 =$

④ $20 \div 5 =$ ⑭ $5 \div 5 =$ ㉔ $30 \div 5 =$

⑤ $25 \div 5 =$ ⑮ $15 \div 5 =$ ㉕ $35 \div 5 =$

⑥ $30 \div 5 =$ ⑯ $25 \div 5 =$ ㉖ $10 \div 5 =$

⑦ $35 \div 5 =$ ⑰ $35 \div 5 =$ ㉗ $25 \div 5 =$

⑧ $40 \div 5 =$ ⑱ $45 \div 5 =$ ㉘ $45 \div 5 =$

⑨ $45 \div 5 =$ ⑲ $10 \div 5 =$ ㉙ $15 \div 5 =$

⑩ $10 \div 5 =$ ⑳ $25 \div 5 =$ ㉚ $30 \div 5 =$

Your Time

min.   sec.

Score

/39

1 Read each number sentence aloud. Trace each answer.

① $6 \div 6 = 1$ ④ $24 \div 6 = 4$ ⑦ $42 \div 6 = 7$

② $12 \div 6 = 2$ ⑤ $30 \div 6 = 5$ ⑧ $48 \div 6 = 8$

③ $18 \div 6 = 3$ ⑥ $36 \div 6 = 6$ ⑨ $54 \div 6 = 9$

2 Divide. Time how long it takes to complete the division problems. Log your time below.

① $6 \div 6 =$ ⑪ $18 \div 6 =$ ㉑ $54 \div 6 =$

② $12 \div 6 =$ ⑫ $30 \div 6 =$ ㉒ $12 \div 6 =$

③ $18 \div 6 =$ ⑬ $42 \div 6 =$ ㉓ $24 \div 6 =$

④ $24 \div 6 =$ ⑭ $54 \div 6 =$ ㉔ $42 \div 6 =$

⑤ $30 \div 6 =$ ⑮ $12 \div 6 =$ ㉕ $18 \div 6 =$

⑥ $36 \div 6 =$ ⑯ $24 \div 6 =$ ㉖ $30 \div 6 =$

⑦ $42 \div 6 =$ ⑰ $36 \div 6 =$ ㉗ $48 \div 6 =$

⑧ $48 \div 6 =$ ⑱ $48 \div 6 =$ ㉘ $6 \div 6 =$

⑨ $54 \div 6 =$ ⑲ $18 \div 6 =$ ㉙ $36 \div 6 =$

⑩ $6 \div 6 =$ ⑳ $6 \div 6 =$ ㉚ $54 \div 6 =$

Your Time

min.   sec.

Score

/39

Date / /   **Name**

1 **Read each number sentence aloud. Trace each answer.**

① $7 \div 7 = 1$ ④ $28 \div 7 = 4$ ⑦ $49 \div 7 = 7$

② $14 \div 7 = 2$ ⑤ $35 \div 7 = 5$ ⑧ $56 \div 7 = 8$

③ $21 \div 7 = 3$ ⑥ $42 \div 7 = 6$ ⑨ $63 \div 7 = 9$

2 **Divide. Time how long it takes to complete the division problems. Log your time below.**

① $7 \div 7 =$ ⑪ $28 \div 7 =$ ㉑ $63 \div 7 =$

② $14 \div 7 =$ ⑫ $42 \div 7 =$ ㉒ $21 \div 7 =$

③ $21 \div 7 =$ ⑬ $56 \div 7 =$ ㉓ $7 \div 7 =$

④ $28 \div 7 =$ ⑭ $7 \div 7 =$ ㉔ $49 \div 7 =$

⑤ $35 \div 7 =$ ⑮ $21 \div 7 =$ ㉕ $42 \div 7 =$

⑥ $42 \div 7 =$ ⑯ $35 \div 7 =$ ㉖ $14 \div 7 =$

⑦ $49 \div 7 =$ ⑰ $49 \div 7 =$ ㉗ $35 \div 7 =$

⑧ $56 \div 7 =$ ⑱ $63 \div 7 =$ ㉘ $56 \div 7 =$

⑨ $63 \div 7 =$ ⑲ $56 \div 7 =$ ㉙ $28 \div 7 =$

⑩ $14 \div 7 =$ ⑳ $28 \div 7 =$ ㉚ $49 \div 7 =$

Your Time

min.   sec.

Score

/39

Date	Name
/ /	

● **Divide. Time how long it takes to complete the division problems. Log your time below.**

① $5 \div 5 =$

② $10 \div 5 =$

③ $15 \div 5 =$

④ $20 \div 5 =$

⑤ $25 \div 5 =$

⑥ $30 \div 5 =$

⑦ $35 \div 5 =$

⑧ $40 \div 5 =$

⑨ $45 \div 5 =$

⑩ $6 \div 6 =$

⑪ $12 \div 6 =$

⑫ $18 \div 6 =$

⑬ $24 \div 6 =$

⑭ $30 \div 6 =$

⑮ $36 \div 6 =$

⑯ $42 \div 6 =$

⑰ $48 \div 6 =$

⑱ $54 \div 6 =$

⑲ $7 \div 7 =$

⑳ $14 \div 7 =$

㉑ $21 \div 7 =$

㉒ $28 \div 7 =$

㉓ $35 \div 7 =$

㉔ $42 \div 7 =$

㉕ $49 \div 7 =$

㉖ $56 \div 7 =$

㉗ $63 \div 7 =$

㉘ $25 \div 5 =$

㉙ $6 \div 6 =$

㉚ $63 \div 7 =$

㉛ $20 \div 5 =$

㉜ $30 \div 6 =$

㉝ $21 \div 7 =$

㉞ $35 \div 5 =$

㉟ $12 \div 6 =$

㊱ $56 \div 7 =$

㊲ $15 \div 5 =$

㊳ $36 \div 6 =$

㊴ $14 \div 7 =$

㊵ $40 \div 5 =$

㊶ $42 \div 6 =$

㊷ $28 \div 7 =$

㊸ $5 \div 5 =$

㊹ $54 \div 6 =$

㊺ $42 \div 7 =$

Your Time

min. sec.

Score

/45

1 **Read each number sentence aloud. Trace each answer.**

① $8 \div 8 = 1$ ④ $32 \div 8 = 4$ ⑦ $56 \div 8 = 7$

② $16 \div 8 = 2$ ⑤ $40 \div 8 = 5$ ⑧ $64 \div 8 = 8$

③ $24 \div 8 = 3$ ⑥ $48 \div 8 = 6$ ⑨ $72 \div 8 = 9$

2 **Divide. Time how long it takes to complete the division problems. Log your time below.**

① $8 \div 8 =$ ⑪ $24 \div 8 =$ ㉑ $16 \div 8 =$

② $16 \div 8 =$ ⑫ $40 \div 8 =$ ㉒ $32 \div 8 =$

③ $24 \div 8 =$ ⑬ $56 \div 8 =$ ㉓ $72 \div 8 =$

④ $32 \div 8 =$ ⑭ $72 \div 8 =$ ㉔ $24 \div 8 =$

⑤ $40 \div 8 =$ ⑮ $16 \div 8 =$ ㉕ $40 \div 8 =$

⑥ $48 \div 8 =$ ⑯ $32 \div 8 =$ ㉖ $48 \div 8 =$

⑦ $56 \div 8 =$ ⑰ $48 \div 8 =$ ㉗ $8 \div 8 =$

⑧ $64 \div 8 =$ ⑱ $64 \div 8 =$ ㉘ $56 \div 8 =$

⑨ $72 \div 8 =$ ⑲ $8 \div 8 =$ ㉙ $16 \div 8 =$

⑩ $8 \div 8 =$ ⑳ $56 \div 8 =$ ㉚ $64 \div 8 =$

Score

Your Time

min. sec. ___/39

Date / / **Name**

1 Read each number sentence aloud. Trace each answer.

① $9 \div 9 = 1$ ④ $36 \div 9 = 4$ ⑦ $63 \div 9 = 7$

② $18 \div 9 = 2$ ⑤ $45 \div 9 = 5$ ⑧ $72 \div 9 = 8$

③ $27 \div 9 = 3$ ⑥ $54 \div 9 = 6$ ⑨ $81 \div 9 = 9$

2 Divide. Time how long it takes to complete the division problems. Log your time below.

① $9 \div 9 =$ ⑪ $36 \div 9 =$ ㉑ $9 \div 9 =$

② $18 \div 9 =$ ⑫ $54 \div 9 =$ ㉒ $81 \div 9 =$

③ $27 \div 9 =$ ⑬ $72 \div 9 =$ ㉓ $36 \div 9 =$

④ $36 \div 9 =$ ⑭ $9 \div 9 =$ ㉔ $63 \div 9 =$

⑤ $45 \div 9 =$ ⑮ $27 \div 9 =$ ㉕ $27 \div 9 =$

⑥ $54 \div 9 =$ ⑯ $45 \div 9 =$ ㉖ $72 \div 9 =$

⑦ $63 \div 9 =$ ⑰ $63 \div 9 =$ ㉗ $18 \div 9 =$

⑧ $72 \div 9 =$ ⑱ $81 \div 9 =$ ㉘ $54 \div 9 =$

⑨ $81 \div 9 =$ ⑲ $27 \div 9 =$ ㉙ $45 \div 9 =$

⑩ $18 \div 9 =$ ⑳ $54 \div 9 =$ ㉚ $81 \div 9 =$

Your Time   min.   sec.

Score   / 39

Warm-Up
Division ÷ 1

Date / /

Name

1 Read each number sentence aloud. Trace each answer.

① $1 \div 1 = 1$ ④ $4 \div 1 = 4$ ⑦ $7 \div 1 = 7$

② $2 \div 1 = 2$ ⑤ $5 \div 1 = 5$ ⑧ $8 \div 1 = 8$

③ $3 \div 1 = 3$ ⑥ $6 \div 1 = 6$ ⑨ $9 \div 1 = 9$

2 Divide. Time how long it takes to complete the division problems. Log your time below.

① $1 \div 1 =$ ⑪ $3 \div 1 =$ ㉑ $6 \div 1 =$

② $2 \div 1 =$ ⑫ $5 \div 1 =$ ㉒ $3 \div 1 =$

③ $3 \div 1 =$ ⑬ $7 \div 1 =$ ㉓ $8 \div 1 =$

④ $4 \div 1 =$ ⑭ $9 \div 1 =$ ㉔ $9 \div 1 =$

⑤ $5 \div 1 =$ ⑮ $2 \div 1 =$ ㉕ $4 \div 1 =$

⑥ $6 \div 1 =$ ⑯ $4 \div 1 =$ ㉖ $2 \div 1 =$

⑦ $7 \div 1 =$ ⑰ $6 \div 1 =$ ㉗ $7 \div 1 =$

⑧ $8 \div 1 =$ ⑱ $8 \div 1 =$ ㉘ $5 \div 1 =$

⑨ $9 \div 1 =$ ⑲ $5 \div 1 =$ ㉙ $8 \div 1 =$

⑩ $1 \div 1 =$ ⑳ $4 \div 1 =$ ㉚ $1 \div 1 =$

Your Time

min.   sec.

Score

/39

Warm-Up
Review: Division ÷8, ÷9, ÷1

Date _____ / _____ / _____   Name _____

● **Divide. Time how long it takes to complete the division problems. Log your time below.**

① 8 ÷ 8 =

② 16 ÷ 8 =

③ 24 ÷ 8 =

④ 32 ÷ 8 =

⑤ 40 ÷ 8 =

⑥ 48 ÷ 8 =

⑦ 56 ÷ 8 =

⑧ 64 ÷ 8 =

⑨ 72 ÷ 8 =

⑩ 9 ÷ 9 =

⑪ 18 ÷ 9 =

⑫ 27 ÷ 9 =

⑬ 36 ÷ 9 =

⑭ 45 ÷ 9 =

⑮ 54 ÷ 9 =

⑯ 63 ÷ 9 =

⑰ 72 ÷ 9 =

⑱ 81 ÷ 9 =

⑲ 1 ÷ 1 =

⑳ 2 ÷ 1 =

㉑ 3 ÷ 1 =

㉒ 4 ÷ 1 =

㉓ 5 ÷ 1 =

㉔ 6 ÷ 1 =

㉕ 7 ÷ 1 =

㉖ 8 ÷ 1 =

㉗ 9 ÷ 1 =

㉘ 48 ÷ 8 =

㉙ 36 ÷ 9 =

㉚ 9 ÷ 1 =

㉛ 8 ÷ 8 =

㉜ 54 ÷ 9 =

㉝ 8 ÷ 1 =

㉞ 40 ÷ 8 =

㉟ 18 ÷ 9 =

㊱ 6 ÷ 1 =

㊲ 8 ÷ 8 =

㊳ 45 ÷ 9 =

㊴ 2 ÷ 1 =

㊵ 56 ÷ 8 =

㊶ 27 ÷ 9 =

㊷ 1 ÷ 1 =

㊸ 16 ÷ 8 =

㊹ 72 ÷ 9 =

㊺ 4 ÷ 1 =

Your Time _____ min. _____ sec.

Score _____ / 45

Date / /   **Name**

● **Divide. Time how long it takes to complete the division problems. Log your time below.**

① $10 \div 2 =$

② $8 \div 4 =$

③ $21 \div 3 =$

④ $30 \div 5 =$

⑤ $6 \div 2 =$

⑥ $24 \div 4 =$

⑦ $45 \div 5 =$

⑧ $3 \div 3 =$

⑨ $16 \div 2 =$

⑩ $10 \div 5 =$

⑪ $9 \div 3 =$

⑫ $20 \div 4 =$

⑬ $8 \div 2 =$

⑭ $24 \div 3 =$

⑮ $25 \div 5 =$

⑯ $36 \div 4 =$

⑰ $4 \div 2 =$

⑱ $15 \div 3 =$

⑲ $20 \div 5 =$

⑳ $28 \div 4 =$

㉑ $18 \div 2 =$

㉒ $40 \div 5 =$

㉓ $6 \div 3 =$

㉔ $4 \div 4 =$

㉕ $12 \div 2 =$

㉖ $15 \div 5 =$

㉗ $32 \div 4 =$

㉘ $18 \div 3 =$

㉙ $35 \div 5 =$

㉚ $2 \div 2 =$

㉛ $12 \div 4 =$

㉜ $27 \div 3 =$

㉝ $5 \div 5 =$

㉞ $14 \div 2 =$

㉟ $25 \div 5 =$

㊱ $12 \div 3 =$

㊲ $16 \div 4 =$

㊳ $6 \div 2 =$

㊴ $8 \div 4 =$

㊵ $15 \div 3 =$

㊶ $30 \div 5 =$

㊷ $16 \div 2 =$

㊸ $36 \div 4 =$

㊹ $3 \div 3 =$

㊺ $8 \div 2 =$

Review any incorrect answers and remember not to rush.

Your Time

Score

min.   sec.   /45

Target Time

2 / 3 / 4 min.

* Based on your time from the previous page, circle a target time for completing this page.

Date

/ /

Name

● **Divide.**

① 6 ÷ 3 =

② 35 ÷ 5 =

③ 16 ÷ 4 =

④ 16 ÷ 2 =

⑤ 27 ÷ 3 =

⑥ 25 ÷ 5 =

⑦ 2 ÷ 2 =

⑧ 12 ÷ 4 =

⑨ 18 ÷ 3 =

⑩ 8 ÷ 2 =

⑪ 20 ÷ 4 =

⑫ 20 ÷ 5 =

⑬ 9 ÷ 3 =

⑭ 14 ÷ 2 =

⑮ 24 ÷ 4 =

⑯ 15 ÷ 5 =

⑰ 21 ÷ 3 =

⑱ 4 ÷ 4 =

⑲ 4 ÷ 2 =

⑳ 40 ÷ 5 =

㉑ 12 ÷ 3 =

㉒ 12 ÷ 2 =

㉓ 28 ÷ 4 =

㉔ 45 ÷ 5 =

㉕ 3 ÷ 3 =

㉖ 30 ÷ 5 =

㉗ 8 ÷ 4 =

㉘ 10 ÷ 2 =

㉙ 24 ÷ 3 =

㉚ 5 ÷ 5 =

㉛ 36 ÷ 4 =

㉜ 6 ÷ 2 =

㉝ 15 ÷ 3 =

㉞ 10 ÷ 5 =

㉟ 32 ÷ 4 =

㊱ 2 ÷ 2 =

㊲ 6 ÷ 3 =

㊳ 35 ÷ 5 =

㊴ 18 ÷ 2 =

㊵ 12 ÷ 4 =

㊶ 21 ÷ 3 =

㊷ 14 ÷ 2 =

㊸ 20 ÷ 4 =

㊹ 20 ÷ 5 =

㊺ 27 ÷ 3 =

Your Time

min.   sec.

Score

/45

Practice
Division from ÷2 to ÷5

Target Time
2 / 3 / 4 min.
* Based on your time from the previous page, circle a target time for completing this page.

Date
/ /

Name

● **Divide.**

① $36 \div 4 =$

② $10 \div 5 =$

③ $14 \div 2 =$

④ $9 \div 3 =$

⑤ $20 \div 4 =$

⑥ $2 \div 2 =$

⑦ $35 \div 5 =$

⑧ $24 \div 3 =$

⑨ $8 \div 4 =$

⑩ $16 \div 2 =$

⑪ $15 \div 5 =$

⑫ $15 \div 3 =$

⑬ $28 \div 4 =$

⑭ $8 \div 2 =$

⑮ $18 \div 3 =$

⑯ $45 \div 5 =$

⑰ $16 \div 4 =$

⑱ $6 \div 3 =$

⑲ $10 \div 2 =$

⑳ $5 \div 5 =$

㉑ $32 \div 4 =$

㉒ $12 \div 2 =$

㉓ $20 \div 5 =$

㉔ $21 \div 3 =$

㉕ $12 \div 4 =$

㉖ $3 \div 3 =$

㉗ $40 \div 5 =$

㉘ $18 \div 2 =$

㉙ $24 \div 4 =$

㉚ $12 \div 3 =$

㉛ $25 \div 5 =$

㉜ $6 \div 2 =$

㉝ $4 \div 4 =$

㉞ $30 \div 5 =$

㉟ $27 \div 3 =$

㊱ $10 \div 2 =$

㊲ $28 \div 4 =$

㊳ $9 \div 3 =$

㊴ $10 \div 5 =$

㊵ $4 \div 2 =$

㊶ $16 \div 4 =$

㊷ $45 \div 5 =$

㊸ $12 \div 2 =$

㊹ $12 \div 3 =$

㊺ $32 \div 4 =$

Your Time

min.   sec.

Score

/45

16
Practice
Division from ÷2 to ÷5

Target Time
2 / 3 / 4 min.
* Based on your time from the previous page,
circle a target time for completing this page.

Date   /   /   Name

● **Divide.**

① $15 \div 5 =$

② $4 \div 4 =$

③ $14 \div 2 =$

④ $6 \div 3 =$

⑤ $20 \div 5 =$

⑥ $36 \div 4 =$

⑦ $9 \div 3 =$

⑧ $10 \div 2 =$

⑨ $40 \div 5 =$

⑩ $28 \div 4 =$

⑪ $4 \div 2 =$

⑫ $21 \div 3 =$

⑬ $5 \div 5 =$

⑭ $24 \div 4 =$

⑮ $16 \div 2 =$

⑯ $15 \div 3 =$

⑰ $30 \div 5 =$

⑱ $8 \div 2 =$

⑲ $24 \div 3 =$

⑳ $8 \div 4 =$

㉑ $45 \div 5 =$

㉒ $20 \div 4 =$

㉓ $6 \div 2 =$

㉔ $12 \div 3 =$

㉕ $10 \div 5 =$

㉖ $12 \div 2 =$

㉗ $3 \div 3 =$

㉘ $12 \div 4 =$

㉙ $25 \div 5 =$

㉚ $18 \div 3 =$

㉛ $18 \div 2 =$

㉜ $32 \div 4 =$

㉝ $35 \div 5 =$

㉞ $16 \div 4 =$

㉟ $2 \div 2 =$

㊱ $27 \div 3 =$

㊲ $15 \div 5 =$

㊳ $24 \div 4 =$

㊴ $4 \div 2 =$

㊵ $24 \div 3 =$

㊶ $5 \div 5 =$

㊷ $18 \div 2 =$

㊸ $4 \div 4 =$

㊹ $18 \div 3 =$

㊺ $40 \div 5 =$

Score

Your Time

min.   sec.   /45

Practice
Division from ÷2 to ÷5

Target Time
2 / 3 / 4 min.
* Based on your time from the previous page, circle a target time for completing this page.

Date	Name
/ /	

● **Divide.**

① $14 \div 2 =$

② $20 \div 5 =$

③ $8 \div 4 =$

④ $18 \div 3 =$

⑤ $6 \div 2 =$

⑥ $5 \div 5 =$

⑦ $24 \div 3 =$

⑧ $36 \div 4 =$

⑨ $12 \div 2 =$

⑩ $6 \div 3 =$

⑪ $28 \div 4 =$

⑫ $40 \div 5 =$

⑬ $10 \div 2 =$

⑭ $16 \div 4 =$

⑮ $10 \div 5 =$

⑯ $3 \div 3 =$

⑰ $18 \div 2 =$

⑱ $30 \div 5 =$

⑲ $12 \div 4 =$

⑳ $21 \div 3 =$

㉑ $8 \div 2 =$

㉒ $25 \div 5 =$

㉓ $9 \div 3 =$

㉔ $24 \div 4 =$

㉕ $2 \div 2 =$

㉖ $20 \div 4 =$

㉗ $12 \div 3 =$

㉘ $45 \div 5 =$

㉙ $4 \div 2 =$

㉚ $32 \div 4 =$

㉛ $15 \div 5 =$

㉜ $15 \div 3 =$

㉝ $16 \div 2 =$

㉞ $4 \div 4 =$

㉟ $35 \div 5 =$

㊱ $27 \div 3 =$

㊲ $6 \div 2 =$

㊳ $8 \div 4 =$

㊴ $5 \div 5 =$

㊵ $12 \div 3 =$

㊶ $14 \div 2 =$

㊷ $40 \div 5 =$

㊸ $6 \div 3 =$

㊹ $36 \div 4 =$

㊺ $12 \div 2 =$

Your Time	Score
min. sec.	/45

Practice
Division from ÷2 to ÷5

Target Time
2 / 3 / 4 min.
* Based on your time from the previous page,
circle a target time for completing this page.

Date   /   /   Name

● **Divide.**

① 24 ÷ 3 =

② 8 ÷ 2 =

③ 12 ÷ 4 =

④ 5 ÷ 5 =

⑤ 6 ÷ 3 =

⑥ 24 ÷ 4 =

⑦ 18 ÷ 2 =

⑧ 35 ÷ 5 =

⑨ 15 ÷ 3 =

⑩ 8 ÷ 4 =

⑪ 6 ÷ 2 =

⑫ 20 ÷ 5 =

⑬ 3 ÷ 3 =

⑭ 45 ÷ 5 =

⑮ 14 ÷ 2 =

⑯ 20 ÷ 4 =

⑰ 12 ÷ 3 =

⑱ 32 ÷ 4 =

⑲ 15 ÷ 5 =

⑳ 4 ÷ 2 =

㉑ 27 ÷ 3 =

㉒ 30 ÷ 5 =

㉓ 4 ÷ 4 =

㉔ 10 ÷ 2 =

㉕ 21 ÷ 3 =

㉖ 10 ÷ 5 =

㉗ 12 ÷ 2 =

㉘ 16 ÷ 4 =

㉙ 9 ÷ 3 =

㉚ 16 ÷ 2 =

㉛ 25 ÷ 5 =

㉜ 28 ÷ 4 =

㉝ 18 ÷ 3 =

㉞ 2 ÷ 2 =

㉟ 40 ÷ 5 =

㊱ 36 ÷ 4 =

㊲ 6 ÷ 3 =

㊳ 8 ÷ 2 =

㊴ 35 ÷ 5 =

㊵ 12 ÷ 4 =

㊶ 15 ÷ 3 =

㊷ 18 ÷ 2 =

㊸ 24 ÷ 4 =

㊹ 5 ÷ 5 =

㊺ 24 ÷ 3 =

Your Time

min.   sec.

Score

/45

19

Practice

Division from ÷2 to ÷5

Target Time
2 / **3** / **4** min.
* Based on your time from the previous page, circle a target time for completing this page.

Date / / **Name**

● **Divide.**

① 12 ÷ 4 =
② 25 ÷ 5 =
③ 12 ÷ 2 =
④ 27 ÷ 3 =
⑤ 16 ÷ 4 =
⑥ 6 ÷ 2 =
⑦ 40 ÷ 5 =
⑧ 9 ÷ 3 =
⑨ 24 ÷ 4 =
⑩ 15 ÷ 5 =
⑪ 2 ÷ 2 =
⑫ 15 ÷ 3 =
⑬ 8 ÷ 4 =
⑭ 35 ÷ 5 =
⑮ 18 ÷ 2 =

⑯ 3 ÷ 3 =
⑰ 32 ÷ 4 =
⑱ 21 ÷ 3 =
⑲ 20 ÷ 5 =
⑳ 16 ÷ 2 =
㉑ 20 ÷ 4 =
㉒ 4 ÷ 2 =
㉓ 12 ÷ 3 =
㉔ 30 ÷ 5 =
㉕ 4 ÷ 4 =
㉖ 6 ÷ 3 =
㉗ 14 ÷ 2 =
㉘ 10 ÷ 5 =
㉙ 36 ÷ 4 =
㉚ 8 ÷ 2 =

㉛ 18 ÷ 3 =
㉜ 45 ÷ 5 =
㉝ 28 ÷ 4 =
㉞ 5 ÷ 5 =
㉟ 10 ÷ 2 =
㊱ 24 ÷ 3 =
㊲ 16 ÷ 4 =
㊳ 3 ÷ 3 =
㊴ 25 ÷ 5 =
㊵ 6 ÷ 2 =
㊶ 32 ÷ 4 =
㊷ 2 ÷ 2 =
㊸ 15 ÷ 5 =
㊹ 27 ÷ 3 =
㊺ 8 ÷ 4 =

Your Time min. sec.

Score /45

Target Time

2 / **3** / **4** min.

* Based on your time from the previous page, circle a target time for completing this page.

Date / /

Name

● **Divide.**

① $30 \div 5 =$

② $6 \div 3 =$

③ $18 \div 2 =$

④ $4 \div 4 =$

⑤ $40 \div 5 =$

⑥ $24 \div 4 =$

⑦ $8 \div 2 =$

⑧ $18 \div 3 =$

⑨ $15 \div 5 =$

⑩ $10 \div 2 =$

⑪ $36 \div 4 =$

⑫ $24 \div 3 =$

⑬ $5 \div 5 =$

⑭ $16 \div 4 =$

⑮ $14 \div 2 =$

⑯ $27 \div 3 =$

⑰ $25 \div 5 =$

⑱ $6 \div 2 =$

⑲ $32 \div 4 =$

⑳ $12 \div 3 =$

㉑ $45 \div 5 =$

㉒ $21 \div 3 =$

㉓ $2 \div 2 =$

㉔ $12 \div 4 =$

㉕ $10 \div 5 =$

㉖ $20 \div 4 =$

㉗ $12 \div 2 =$

㉘ $9 \div 3 =$

㉙ $35 \div 5 =$

㉚ $8 \div 4 =$

㉛ $15 \div 3 =$

㉜ $16 \div 2 =$

㉝ $20 \div 5 =$

㉞ $3 \div 3 =$

㉟ $28 \div 4 =$

㊱ $4 \div 2 =$

㊲ $40 \div 5 =$

㊳ $12 \div 3 =$

㊴ $10 \div 2 =$

㊵ $36 \div 4 =$

㊶ $30 \div 5 =$

㊷ $4 \div 4 =$

㊸ $14 \div 2 =$

㊹ $9 \div 3 =$

㊺ $45 \div 5 =$

Your Time

min. sec.

Score

/45

Practice
Division from ÷2 to ÷5

Target Time

2 / 3 / 4 min.

* Based on your time from the previous page, circle a target time for completing this page.

Date / /

Name

● **Divide.**

① $8 \div 2 =$

② $25 \div 5 =$

③ $18 \div 3 =$

④ $4 \div 4 =$

⑤ $4 \div 2 =$

⑥ $15 \div 5 =$

⑦ $12 \div 3 =$

⑧ $20 \div 4 =$

⑨ $14 \div 2 =$

⑩ $30 \div 5 =$

⑪ $27 \div 3 =$

⑫ $28 \div 4 =$

⑬ $16 \div 2 =$

⑭ $6 \div 3 =$

⑮ $40 \div 5 =$

⑯ $16 \div 4 =$

⑰ $6 \div 2 =$

⑱ $32 \div 4 =$

⑲ $15 \div 3 =$

⑳ $45 \div 5 =$

㉑ $12 \div 2 =$

㉒ $8 \div 4 =$

㉓ $21 \div 3 =$

㉔ $20 \div 5 =$

㉕ $18 \div 2 =$

㉖ $3 \div 3 =$

㉗ $35 \div 5 =$

㉘ $12 \div 4 =$

㉙ $2 \div 2 =$

㉚ $10 \div 5 =$

㉛ $24 \div 3 =$

㉜ $24 \div 4 =$

㉝ $10 \div 2 =$

㉞ $5 \div 5 =$

㉟ $9 \div 3 =$

㊱ $36 \div 4 =$

㊲ $16 \div 2 =$

㊳ $20 \div 5 =$

㊴ $18 \div 3 =$

㊵ $28 \div 4 =$

㊶ $4 \div 2 =$

㊷ $10 \div 5 =$

㊸ $20 \div 4 =$

㊹ $21 \div 3 =$

㊺ $12 \div 2 =$

Score

Your Time

min.　　sec.

/45

22

Practice
Division from ÷2 to ÷5

Target Time

2 / 3 / 4 min.

* Based on your time from the previous page,
circle a target time for completing this page.

Date

Name

/   /

● **Divide.**

① 3 ÷ 3 =

② 32 ÷ 4 =

③ 8 ÷ 2 =

④ 10 ÷ 5 =

⑤ 12 ÷ 3 =

⑥ 40 ÷ 5 =

⑦ 24 ÷ 4 =

⑧ 18 ÷ 2 =

⑨ 21 ÷ 3 =

⑩ 15 ÷ 5 =

⑪ 16 ÷ 4 =

⑫ 2 ÷ 2 =

⑬ 27 ÷ 3 =

⑭ 12 ÷ 4 =

⑮ 35 ÷ 5 =

⑯ 10 ÷ 2 =

⑰ 6 ÷ 3 =

⑱ 6 ÷ 2 =

⑲ 28 ÷ 4 =

⑳ 20 ÷ 5 =

㉑ 15 ÷ 3 =

㉒ 12 ÷ 2 =

㉓ 4 ÷ 4 =

㉔ 30 ÷ 5 =

㉕ 14 ÷ 2 =

㉖ 24 ÷ 3 =

㉗ 4 ÷ 2 =

㉘ 25 ÷ 5 =

㉙ 36 ÷ 4 =

㉚ 9 ÷ 3 =

㉛ 20 ÷ 4 =

㉜ 5 ÷ 5 =

㉝ 16 ÷ 2 =

㉞ 18 ÷ 3 =

㉟ 8 ÷ 4 =

㊱ 45 ÷ 5 =

㊲ 6 ÷ 2 =

㊳ 12 ÷ 3 =

㊴ 32 ÷ 4 =

㊵ 10 ÷ 5 =

㊶ 10 ÷ 2 =

㊷ 27 ÷ 3 =

㊸ 15 ÷ 5 =

㊹ 24 ÷ 4 =

㊺ 3 ÷ 3 =

Your Time

min.   sec.

Score

/45

Practice
Division from ÷2 to ÷5

Target Time
2 / 3 / 4 min.
* Based on your time from the previous page,
circle a target time for completing this page.

Date

Name

/ /

● **Divide.**

① 28 ÷ 4 =

② 9 ÷ 3 =

③ 25 ÷ 5 =

④ 18 ÷ 2 =

⑤ 16 ÷ 4 =

⑥ 12 ÷ 2 =

⑦ 40 ÷ 5 =

⑧ 15 ÷ 3 =

⑨ 8 ÷ 4 =

⑩ 5 ÷ 5 =

⑪ 18 ÷ 3 =

⑫ 6 ÷ 2 =

⑬ 4 ÷ 4 =

⑭ 12 ÷ 3 =

⑮ 45 ÷ 5 =

⑯ 16 ÷ 2 =

⑰ 20 ÷ 4 =

⑱ 6 ÷ 3 =

⑲ 15 ÷ 5 =

⑳ 8 ÷ 2 =

㉑ 36 ÷ 4 =

㉒ 3 ÷ 3 =

㉓ 30 ÷ 5 =

㉔ 14 ÷ 2 =

㉕ 12 ÷ 4 =

㉖ 10 ÷ 2 =

㉗ 21 ÷ 3 =

㉘ 10 ÷ 5 =

㉙ 24 ÷ 4 =

㉚ 24 ÷ 3 =

㉛ 2 ÷ 2 =

㉜ 35 ÷ 5 =

㉝ 32 ÷ 4 =

㉞ 4 ÷ 2 =

㉟ 27 ÷ 3 =

㊱ 20 ÷ 5 =

㊲ 4 ÷ 4 =

㊳ 12 ÷ 2 =

㊴ 40 ÷ 5 =

㊵ 9 ÷ 3 =

㊶ 16 ÷ 4 =

㊷ 15 ÷ 3 =

㊸ 14 ÷ 2 =

㊹ 45 ÷ 5 =

㊺ 8 ÷ 4 =

Your Time

min.   sec.

Score

/45

Practice
Division from ÷2 to ÷5

Target Time

2 / **3** / **4** min.

* Based on your time from the previous page, circle a target time for completing this page.

Date	Name
/ /	

● **Divide.**

① $25 \div 5 =$

② $18 \div 3 =$

③ $16 \div 4 =$

④ $6 \div 2 =$

⑤ $45 \div 5 =$

⑥ $3 \div 3 =$

⑦ $10 \div 2 =$

⑧ $32 \div 4 =$

⑨ $20 \div 5 =$

⑩ $18 \div 2 =$

⑪ $28 \div 4 =$

⑫ $15 \div 3 =$

⑬ $10 \div 5 =$

⑭ $12 \div 2 =$

⑮ $24 \div 3 =$

⑯ $4 \div 4 =$

⑰ $35 \div 5 =$

⑱ $6 \div 3 =$

⑲ $8 \div 2 =$

⑳ $36 \div 4 =$

㉑ $40 \div 5 =$

㉒ $8 \div 4 =$

㉓ $2 \div 2 =$

㉔ $21 \div 3 =$

㉕ $15 \div 5 =$

㉖ $12 \div 3 =$

㉗ $20 \div 4 =$

㉘ $4 \div 2 =$

㉙ $30 \div 5 =$

㉚ $9 \div 3 =$

㉛ $16 \div 2 =$

㉜ $24 \div 4 =$

㉝ $5 \div 5 =$

㉞ $14 \div 2 =$

㉟ $12 \div 4 =$

㊱ $27 \div 3 =$

㊲ $25 \div 5 =$

㊳ $8 \div 2 =$

㊴ $36 \div 4 =$

㊵ $18 \div 3 =$

㊶ $35 \div 5 =$

㊷ $24 \div 3 =$

㊸ $20 \div 4 =$

㊹ $18 \div 2 =$

㊺ $20 \div 5 =$

Your Time		Score
min.	sec.	/45

Practice
Division from ÷2 to ÷5

Target Time
2 / 3 / 4 min.
* Based on your time from the previous page, circle a target time for completing this page.

Date / /   **Name**

● **Divide.**

① 12 ÷ 2 =

② 3 ÷ 3 =

③ 16 ÷ 4 =

④ 15 ÷ 5 =

⑤ 4 ÷ 2 =

⑥ 18 ÷ 3 =

⑦ 36 ÷ 4 =

⑧ 25 ÷ 5 =

⑨ 14 ÷ 2 =

⑩ 12 ÷ 4 =

⑪ 6 ÷ 3 =

⑫ 30 ÷ 5 =

⑬ 8 ÷ 2 =

⑭ 4 ÷ 4 =

⑮ 21 ÷ 3 =

⑯ 10 ÷ 5 =

⑰ 2 ÷ 2 =

⑱ 9 ÷ 3 =

⑲ 24 ÷ 4 =

⑳ 20 ÷ 5 =

㉑ 10 ÷ 2 =

㉒ 27 ÷ 3 =

㉓ 8 ÷ 4 =

㉔ 45 ÷ 5 =

㉕ 16 ÷ 2 =

㉖ 5 ÷ 5 =

㉗ 15 ÷ 3 =

㉘ 32 ÷ 4 =

㉙ 6 ÷ 2 =

㉚ 28 ÷ 4 =

㉛ 24 ÷ 3 =

㉜ 35 ÷ 5 =

㉝ 18 ÷ 2 =

㉞ 12 ÷ 3 =

㉟ 20 ÷ 4 =

㊱ 40 ÷ 5 =

㊲ 4 ÷ 2 =

㊳ 12 ÷ 4 =

㊴ 21 ÷ 3 =

㊵ 30 ÷ 5 =

㊶ 2 ÷ 2 =

㊷ 5 ÷ 5 =

㊸ 28 ÷ 4 =

㊹ 6 ÷ 3 =

㊺ 16 ÷ 2 =

Your Time

min.   sec.

Score

/45

Practice
Division from ÷2 to ÷5

Target Time

2 / 3 / 4 min.

* Based on your time from the previous page, circle a target time for completing this page.

Date	Name
/ /	

● **Divide.**

① 12 ÷ 3 =

② 35 ÷ 5 =

③ 8 ÷ 2 =

④ 8 ÷ 4 =

⑤ 21 ÷ 3 =

⑥ 20 ÷ 5 =

⑦ 14 ÷ 2 =

⑧ 20 ÷ 4 =

⑨ 24 ÷ 3 =

⑩ 5 ÷ 5 =

⑪ 6 ÷ 2 =

⑫ 36 ÷ 4 =

⑬ 6 ÷ 3 =

⑭ 12 ÷ 2 =

⑮ 45 ÷ 5 =

⑯ 32 ÷ 4 =

⑰ 18 ÷ 3 =

⑱ 10 ÷ 5 =

⑲ 16 ÷ 4 =

⑳ 2 ÷ 2 =

㉑ 9 ÷ 3 =

㉒ 40 ÷ 5 =

㉓ 28 ÷ 4 =

㉔ 10 ÷ 2 =

㉕ 27 ÷ 3 =

㉖ 30 ÷ 5 =

㉗ 18 ÷ 2 =

㉘ 4 ÷ 4 =

㉙ 15 ÷ 3 =

㉚ 15 ÷ 5 =

㉛ 24 ÷ 4 =

㉜ 4 ÷ 2 =

㉝ 3 ÷ 3 =

㉞ 25 ÷ 5 =

㉟ 12 ÷ 4 =

㊱ 16 ÷ 2 =

㊲ 21 ÷ 3 =

㊳ 12 ÷ 2 =

㊴ 20 ÷ 5 =

㊵ 20 ÷ 4 =

㊶ 6 ÷ 3 =

㊷ 6 ÷ 2 =

㊸ 36 ÷ 4 =

㊹ 5 ÷ 5 =

㊺ 18 ÷ 3 =

Your Time	Score
min. sec.	/45

27

Practice
Division from ÷6 to ÷9, ÷1

Target Time
2 / 3 / 4 min.
* Based on your time from the previous page, circle a target time for completing this page.

Date   /   /   Name

● **Divide.**

① 30 ÷ 6 =

② 56 ÷ 8 =

③ 9 ÷ 9 =

④ 63 ÷ 7 =

⑤ 7 ÷ 1 =

⑥ 12 ÷ 6 =

⑦ 40 ÷ 8 =

⑧ 42 ÷ 7 =

⑨ 2 ÷ 1 =

⑩ 36 ÷ 9 =

⑪ 48 ÷ 6 =

⑫ 21 ÷ 7 =

⑬ 5 ÷ 1 =

⑭ 54 ÷ 9 =

⑮ 8 ÷ 8 =

⑯ 18 ÷ 6 =

⑰ 8 ÷ 1 =

⑱ 35 ÷ 7 =

⑲ 63 ÷ 9 =

⑳ 16 ÷ 8 =

㉑ 54 ÷ 6 =

㉒ 4 ÷ 1 =

㉓ 27 ÷ 9 =

㉔ 7 ÷ 7 =

㉕ 6 ÷ 1 =

㉖ 42 ÷ 6 =

㉗ 81 ÷ 9 =

㉘ 32 ÷ 8 =

㉙ 56 ÷ 7 =

㉚ 1 ÷ 1 =

㉛ 36 ÷ 6 =

㉜ 72 ÷ 9 =

㉝ 72 ÷ 8 =

㉞ 28 ÷ 7 =

㉟ 9 ÷ 1 =

㊱ 6 ÷ 6 =

㊲ 64 ÷ 8 =

㊳ 18 ÷ 9 =

㊴ 49 ÷ 7 =

㊵ 3 ÷ 1 =

㊶ 24 ÷ 6 =

㊷ 24 ÷ 8 =

㊸ 48 ÷ 8 =

㊹ 14 ÷ 7 =

㊺ 45 ÷ 9 =

Score

Your Time

min.   sec.   /45

Practice
Division from ÷6 to ÷9, ÷1

Target Time
2 / 3 / 4 min.
* Based on your time from the previous page,
circle a target time for completing this page.

Date   /   /

Name

● **Divide.**

① 49 ÷ 7 =

② 2 ÷ 1 =

③ 40 ÷ 8 =

④ 9 ÷ 9 =

⑤ 36 ÷ 6 =

⑥ 21 ÷ 7 =

⑦ 64 ÷ 8 =

⑧ 54 ÷ 6 =

⑨ 36 ÷ 9 =

⑩ 8 ÷ 1 =

⑪ 63 ÷ 7 =

⑫ 6 ÷ 6 =

⑬ 63 ÷ 9 =

⑭ 24 ÷ 8 =

⑮ 9 ÷ 1 =

⑯ 24 ÷ 6 =

⑰ 14 ÷ 7 =

⑱ 54 ÷ 9 =

⑲ 5 ÷ 1 =

⑳ 32 ÷ 8 =

㉑ 12 ÷ 6 =

㉒ 35 ÷ 7 =

㉓ 27 ÷ 9 =

㉔ 42 ÷ 6 =

㉕ 48 ÷ 8 =

㉖ 4 ÷ 1 =

㉗ 56 ÷ 7 =

㉘ 8 ÷ 8 =

㉙ 7 ÷ 1 =

㉚ 18 ÷ 9 =

㉛ 48 ÷ 6 =

㉜ 7 ÷ 7 =

㉝ 56 ÷ 8 =

㉞ 6 ÷ 1 =

㉟ 81 ÷ 9 =

㊱ 28 ÷ 7 =

㊲ 3 ÷ 1 =

㊳ 72 ÷ 9 =

㊴ 16 ÷ 8 =

㊵ 30 ÷ 6 =

㊶ 42 ÷ 7 =

㊷ 18 ÷ 6 =

㊸ 45 ÷ 9 =

㊹ 1 ÷ 1 =

㊺ 72 ÷ 8 =

Your Time

min.   sec.

Score

/45

Practice
Division from ÷6 to ÷9, ÷1

Target Time

2 / 3 / 4 min.

* Based on your time from the previous page, circle a target time for completing this page.

Date / /

Name

● **Divide.**

① $16 \div 8 =$

② $63 \div 9 =$

③ $30 \div 6 =$

④ $3 \div 1 =$

⑤ $48 \div 8 =$

⑥ $28 \div 7 =$

⑦ $9 \div 9 =$

⑧ $42 \div 6 =$

⑨ $6 \div 1 =$

⑩ $32 \div 8 =$

⑪ $21 \div 7 =$

⑫ $7 \div 1 =$

⑬ $12 \div 6 =$

⑭ $45 \div 9 =$

⑮ $56 \div 7 =$

⑯ $72 \div 8 =$

⑰ $1 \div 1 =$

⑱ $36 \div 9 =$

⑲ $36 \div 6 =$

⑳ $14 \div 7 =$

㉑ $40 \div 8 =$

㉒ $18 \div 6 =$

㉓ $9 \div 1 =$

㉔ $54 \div 9 =$

㉕ $6 \div 6 =$

㉖ $64 \div 8 =$

㉗ $63 \div 7 =$

㉘ $18 \div 9 =$

㉙ $5 \div 1 =$

㉚ $54 \div 6 =$

㉛ $49 \div 7 =$

㉜ $24 \div 8 =$

㉝ $8 \div 1 =$

㉞ $81 \div 9 =$

㉟ $7 \div 7 =$

㊱ $24 \div 6 =$

㊲ $56 \div 8 =$

㊳ $2 \div 1 =$

㊴ $35 \div 7 =$

㊵ $27 \div 9 =$

㊶ $48 \div 6 =$

㊷ $8 \div 8 =$

㊸ $42 \div 7 =$

㊹ $72 \div 9 =$

㊺ $4 \div 1 =$

Your Time

min.   sec.

Score

/45

Practice
Division from ÷6 to ÷9, ÷1

Target Time
2 / 3 / 4 min.
* Based on your time from the previous page, circle a target time for completing this page.

Date / /

Name

● **Divide.**

① $36 \div 9 =$

② $49 \div 7 =$

③ $72 \div 8 =$

④ $48 \div 6 =$

⑤ $6 \div 1 =$

⑥ $9 \div 9 =$

⑦ $30 \div 6 =$

⑧ $64 \div 8 =$

⑨ $9 \div 1 =$

⑩ $21 \div 7 =$

⑪ $63 \div 9 =$

⑫ $8 \div 8 =$

⑬ $56 \div 7 =$

⑭ $12 \div 6 =$

⑮ $3 \div 1 =$

⑯ $45 \div 9 =$

⑰ $54 \div 6 =$

⑱ $1 \div 1 =$

⑲ $28 \div 7 =$

⑳ $16 \div 8 =$

㉑ $27 \div 9 =$

㉒ $7 \div 1 =$

㉓ $7 \div 7 =$

㉔ $36 \div 6 =$

㉕ $32 \div 8 =$

㉖ $72 \div 9 =$

㉗ $5 \div 1 =$

㉘ $18 \div 6 =$

㉙ $40 \div 8 =$

㉚ $14 \div 7 =$

㉛ $54 \div 9 =$

㉜ $24 \div 8 =$

㉝ $42 \div 6 =$

㉞ $35 \div 7 =$

㉟ $2 \div 1 =$

㊱ $81 \div 9 =$

㊲ $4 \div 1 =$

㊳ $6 \div 6 =$

㊴ $63 \div 7 =$

㊵ $48 \div 8 =$

㊶ $18 \div 9 =$

㊷ $8 \div 1 =$

㊸ $42 \div 7 =$

㊹ $24 \div 6 =$

㊺ $56 \div 8 =$

Score

Your Time

min.   sec.   /45

Practice
Division from ÷6 to ÷9, ÷1

Target Time
2 / 3 / 4 min.
* Based on your time from the previous page, circle a target time for completing this page.

Date / / **Name**

● **Divide.**

① 8 ÷ 1 =

② 54 ÷ 9 =

③ 6 ÷ 6 =

④ 21 ÷ 7 =

⑤ 5 ÷ 1 =

⑥ 16 ÷ 8 =

⑦ 63 ÷ 9 =

⑧ 28 ÷ 7 =

⑨ 36 ÷ 6 =

⑩ 72 ÷ 8 =

⑪ 2 ÷ 1 =

⑫ 24 ÷ 8 =

⑬ 54 ÷ 6 =

⑭ 9 ÷ 9 =

⑮ 35 ÷ 7 =

⑯ 4 ÷ 1 =

⑰ 64 ÷ 8 =

⑱ 42 ÷ 7 =

⑲ 18 ÷ 6 =

⑳ 72 ÷ 9 =

㉑ 32 ÷ 8 =

㉒ 7 ÷ 1 =

㉓ 81 ÷ 9 =

㉔ 12 ÷ 6 =

㉕ 56 ÷ 7 =

㉖ 40 ÷ 8 =

㉗ 1 ÷ 1 =

㉘ 27 ÷ 9 =

㉙ 63 ÷ 7 =

㉚ 56 ÷ 8 =

㉛ 42 ÷ 6 =

㉜ 6 ÷ 1 =

㉝ 14 ÷ 7 =

㉞ 8 ÷ 8 =

㉟ 30 ÷ 6 =

㊱ 36 ÷ 9 =

㊲ 3 ÷ 1 =

㊳ 49 ÷ 7 =

㊴ 18 ÷ 9 =

㊵ 48 ÷ 8 =

㊶ 24 ÷ 6 =

㊷ 9 ÷ 1 =

㊸ 7 ÷ 7 =

㊹ 48 ÷ 6 =

㊺ 45 ÷ 9 =

Score

Your Time

min.   sec.

/45

32

Practice
Division from ÷6 to ÷9, ÷1

Target Time

2 / **3** / **4** min.

* Based on your time from the previous page, circle a target time for completing this page.

Date   /   /   **Name**

● **Divide.**

① $18 \div 6 =$

② $56 \div 7 =$

③ $36 \div 9 =$

④ $7 \div 1 =$

⑤ $8 \div 8 =$

⑥ $54 \div 6 =$

⑦ $45 \div 9 =$

⑧ $49 \div 7 =$

⑨ $2 \div 1 =$

⑩ $24 \div 8 =$

⑪ $30 \div 6 =$

⑫ $72 \div 9 =$

⑬ $4 \div 1 =$

⑭ $14 \div 7 =$

⑮ $48 \div 8 =$

⑯ $6 \div 6 =$

⑰ $35 \div 7 =$

⑱ $8 \div 1 =$

⑲ $32 \div 8 =$

⑳ $27 \div 9 =$

㉑ $42 \div 6 =$

㉒ $9 \div 1 =$

㉓ $16 \div 8 =$

㉔ $54 \div 9 =$

㉕ $7 \div 7 =$

㉖ $24 \div 6 =$

㉗ $3 \div 1 =$

㉘ $42 \div 7 =$

㉙ $72 \div 8 =$

㉚ $63 \div 9 =$

㉛ $48 \div 6 =$

㉜ $1 \div 1 =$

㉝ $81 \div 9 =$

㉞ $28 \div 7 =$

㉟ $64 \div 8 =$

㊱ $12 \div 6 =$

㊲ $5 \div 1 =$

㊳ $63 \div 7 =$

㊴ $9 \div 9 =$

㊵ $56 \div 8 =$

㊶ $36 \div 6 =$

㊷ $40 \div 8 =$

㊸ $21 \div 7 =$

㊹ $6 \div 1 =$

㊺ $18 \div 9 =$

Your Time

min.   sec.

Score

/45

Practice
Division from ÷6 to ÷9, ÷1

Target Time

2 / 3 / 4 min.

* Based on your time from the previous page, circle a target time for completing this page.

Date   /   /   Name

● **Divide.**

① 63 ÷ 7 =

② 16 ÷ 8 =

③ 48 ÷ 6 =

④ 45 ÷ 9 =

⑤ 1 ÷ 1 =

⑥ 56 ÷ 7 =

⑦ 18 ÷ 6 =

⑧ 54 ÷ 9 =

⑨ 40 ÷ 8 =

⑩ 8 ÷ 1 =

⑪ 21 ÷ 7 =

⑫ 36 ÷ 6 =

⑬ 56 ÷ 8 =

⑭ 4 ÷ 1 =

⑮ 9 ÷ 9 =

⑯ 9 ÷ 1 =

⑰ 42 ÷ 7 =

⑱ 12 ÷ 6 =

⑲ 27 ÷ 9 =

⑳ 72 ÷ 8 =

㉑ 6 ÷ 1 =

㉒ 28 ÷ 7 =

㉓ 54 ÷ 6 =

㉔ 3 ÷ 1 =

㉕ 8 ÷ 8 =

㉖ 63 ÷ 9 =

㉗ 14 ÷ 7 =

㉘ 24 ÷ 6 =

㉙ 81 ÷ 9 =

㉚ 64 ÷ 8 =

㉛ 35 ÷ 7 =

㉜ 7 ÷ 1 =

㉝ 24 ÷ 8 =

㉞ 30 ÷ 6 =

㉟ 36 ÷ 9 =

㊱ 7 ÷ 7 =

㊲ 42 ÷ 6 =

㊳ 48 ÷ 8 =

㊴ 18 ÷ 9 =

㊵ 5 ÷ 1 =

㊶ 49 ÷ 7 =

㊷ 6 ÷ 6 =

㊸ 32 ÷ 8 =

㊹ 2 ÷ 1 =

㊺ 72 ÷ 9 =

Your Time   min.   sec.

Score   / 45

Practice
Division from ÷6 to ÷9, ÷1

Target Time

2 / 3 / 4 min.

* Based on your time from the previous page, circle a target time for completing this page.

Date / /

Name

● **Divide.**

① 8 ÷ 8 =

② 18 ÷ 6 =

③ 63 ÷ 9 =

④ 5 ÷ 1 =

⑤ 14 ÷ 7 =

⑥ 24 ÷ 8 =

⑦ 54 ÷ 6 =

⑧ 6 ÷ 1 =

⑨ 36 ÷ 9 =

⑩ 49 ÷ 7 =

⑪ 64 ÷ 8 =

⑫ 6 ÷ 6 =

⑬ 21 ÷ 7 =

⑭ 45 ÷ 9 =

⑮ 3 ÷ 1 =

⑯ 40 ÷ 8 =

⑰ 9 ÷ 1 =

⑱ 27 ÷ 9 =

⑲ 63 ÷ 7 =

⑳ 36 ÷ 6 =

㉑ 16 ÷ 8 =

㉒ 28 ÷ 7 =

㉓ 81 ÷ 9 =

㉔ 1 ÷ 1 =

㉕ 56 ÷ 7 =

㉖ 12 ÷ 6 =

㉗ 56 ÷ 8 =

㉘ 4 ÷ 1 =

㉙ 35 ÷ 7 =

㉚ 18 ÷ 9 =

㉛ 48 ÷ 6 =

㉜ 32 ÷ 8 =

㉝ 42 ÷ 7 =

㉞ 9 ÷ 9 =

㉟ 7 ÷ 1 =

㊱ 30 ÷ 6 =

㊲ 48 ÷ 8 =

㊳ 72 ÷ 9 =

㊴ 42 ÷ 6 =

㊵ 2 ÷ 1 =

㊶ 72 ÷ 8 =

㊷ 7 ÷ 7 =

㊸ 24 ÷ 6 =

㊹ 54 ÷ 9 =

㊺ 8 ÷ 1 =

Your Time

min. sec.

Score

/45

Practice
Division from ÷6 to ÷9, ÷1

Target Time
2 / **3** / **4** min.
* Based on your time from the previous page, circle a target time for completing this page.

Date　　　/　　/

Name

● **Divide.**

① 54 ÷ 9 =

② 24 ÷ 8 =

③ 7 ÷ 7 =

④ 5 ÷ 1 =

⑤ 18 ÷ 9 =

⑥ 48 ÷ 6 =

⑦ 42 ÷ 7 =

⑧ 4 ÷ 1 =

⑨ 64 ÷ 8 =

⑩ 6 ÷ 6 =

⑪ 63 ÷ 9 =

⑫ 63 ÷ 7 =

⑬ 48 ÷ 8 =

⑭ 2 ÷ 1 =

⑮ 30 ÷ 6 =

⑯ 56 ÷ 7 =

⑰ 9 ÷ 9 =

⑱ 40 ÷ 8 =

⑲ 14 ÷ 7 =

⑳ 54 ÷ 6 =

㉑ 3 ÷ 1 =

㉒ 45 ÷ 9 =

㉓ 8 ÷ 8 =

㉔ 8 ÷ 1 =

㉕ 35 ÷ 7 =

㉖ 12 ÷ 6 =

㉗ 81 ÷ 9 =

㉘ 56 ÷ 8 =

㉙ 24 ÷ 6 =

㉚ 6 ÷ 1 =

㉛ 36 ÷ 9 =

㉜ 7 ÷ 1 =

㉝ 72 ÷ 8 =

㉞ 18 ÷ 6 =

㉟ 16 ÷ 8 =

㊱ 72 ÷ 9 =

㊲ 21 ÷ 7 =

㊳ 1 ÷ 1 =

㊴ 42 ÷ 6 =

㊵ 32 ÷ 8 =

㊶ 27 ÷ 9 =

㊷ 49 ÷ 7 =

㊸ 9 ÷ 1 =

㊹ 36 ÷ 6 =

㊺ 28 ÷ 7 =

Your Time

min.　　　sec.

Score

/45

36

Practice
Division from ÷6 to ÷9, ÷1

Target Time
2 / 3 / 4 min.
* Based on your time from the previous page, circle a target time for completing this page.

Date   /   /

Name

● **Divide.**

① 7 ÷ 1 =

② 36 ÷ 9 =

③ 6 ÷ 6 =

④ 42 ÷ 7 =

⑤ 64 ÷ 8 =

⑥ 4 ÷ 1 =

⑦ 56 ÷ 7 =

⑧ 18 ÷ 9 =

⑨ 36 ÷ 6 =

⑩ 72 ÷ 8 =

⑪ 2 ÷ 1 =

⑫ 30 ÷ 6 =

⑬ 72 ÷ 9 =

⑭ 56 ÷ 8 =

⑮ 21 ÷ 7 =

⑯ 54 ÷ 9 =

⑰ 9 ÷ 1 =

⑱ 16 ÷ 8 =

⑲ 24 ÷ 6 =

⑳ 35 ÷ 7 =

㉑ 81 ÷ 9 =

㉒ 3 ÷ 1 =

㉓ 24 ÷ 8 =

㉔ 7 ÷ 7 =

㉕ 42 ÷ 6 =

㉖ 27 ÷ 9 =

㉗ 6 ÷ 1 =

㉘ 14 ÷ 7 =

㉙ 54 ÷ 6 =

㉚ 8 ÷ 8 =

㉛ 45 ÷ 9 =

㉜ 1 ÷ 1 =

㉝ 48 ÷ 6 =

㉞ 48 ÷ 8 =

㉟ 28 ÷ 7 =

㊱ 63 ÷ 9 =

㊲ 8 ÷ 1 =

㊳ 12 ÷ 6 =

㊴ 49 ÷ 7 =

㊵ 40 ÷ 8 =

㊶ 9 ÷ 9 =

㊷ 5 ÷ 1 =

㊸ 63 ÷ 7 =

㊹ 32 ÷ 8 =

㊺ 18 ÷ 6 =

Your Time

min.   sec.

Score

/45

37

Practice
Division from ÷6 to ÷9, ÷1

Target Time

2 / 3 / 4 min.

** Based on your time from the previous page,
circle a target time for completing this page.*

Date   /   /

Name

● **Divide.**

① $24 \div 6 =$

② $56 \div 7 =$

③ $63 \div 9 =$

④ $16 \div 8 =$

⑤ $1 \div 1 =$

⑥ $48 \div 6 =$

⑦ $21 \div 7 =$

⑧ $81 \div 9 =$

⑨ $4 \div 1 =$

⑩ $40 \div 8 =$

⑪ $6 \div 6 =$

⑫ $27 \div 9 =$

⑬ $49 \div 7 =$

⑭ $6 \div 1 =$

⑮ $72 \div 8 =$

⑯ $9 \div 9 =$

⑰ $12 \div 6 =$

⑱ $32 \div 8 =$

⑲ $9 \div 1 =$

⑳ $42 \div 7 =$

㉑ $45 \div 9 =$

㉒ $18 \div 6 =$

㉓ $63 \div 7 =$

㉔ $2 \div 1 =$

㉕ $8 \div 8 =$

㉖ $42 \div 6 =$

㉗ $54 \div 9 =$

㉘ $14 \div 7 =$

㉙ $64 \div 8 =$

㉚ $3 \div 1 =$

㉛ $54 \div 6 =$

㉜ $18 \div 9 =$

㉝ $48 \div 8 =$

㉞ $28 \div 7 =$

㉟ $8 \div 1 =$

㊱ $30 \div 6 =$

㊲ $72 \div 9 =$

㊳ $7 \div 7 =$

㊴ $56 \div 8 =$

㊵ $5 \div 1 =$

㊶ $36 \div 6 =$

㊷ $36 \div 9 =$

㊸ $24 \div 8 =$

㊹ $35 \div 7 =$

㊺ $7 \div 1 =$

Your Time

min.   sec.

Score

/45

38

Practice
Division from ÷6 to ÷9, ÷1

Target Time
2 / 3 / 4 min.
* Based on your time from the previous page, circle a target time for completing this page.

Date   /   /

Name

● **Divide.**

① 14 ÷ 7 =

② 42 ÷ 6 =

③ 45 ÷ 9 =

④ 6 ÷ 1 =

⑤ 16 ÷ 8 =

⑥ 63 ÷ 7 =

⑦ 6 ÷ 6 =

⑧ 3 ÷ 1 =

⑨ 32 ÷ 8 =

⑩ 63 ÷ 9 =

⑪ 4 ÷ 1 =

⑫ 35 ÷ 7 =

⑬ 18 ÷ 6 =

⑭ 56 ÷ 8 =

⑮ 81 ÷ 9 =

⑯ 1 ÷ 1 =

⑰ 49 ÷ 7 =

⑱ 48 ÷ 6 =

⑲ 36 ÷ 9 =

⑳ 9 ÷ 1 =

㉑ 21 ÷ 7 =

㉒ 64 ÷ 8 =

㉓ 54 ÷ 6 =

㉔ 18 ÷ 9 =

㉕ 24 ÷ 6 =

㉖ 8 ÷ 8 =

㉗ 56 ÷ 7 =

㉘ 54 ÷ 9 =

㉙ 40 ÷ 8 =

㉚ 2 ÷ 1 =

㉛ 36 ÷ 6 =

㉜ 8 ÷ 1 =

㉝ 7 ÷ 7 =

㉞ 27 ÷ 9 =

㉟ 30 ÷ 6 =

㊱ 48 ÷ 8 =

㊲ 7 ÷ 1 =

㊳ 28 ÷ 7 =

㊴ 72 ÷ 9 =

㊵ 12 ÷ 6 =

㊶ 5 ÷ 1 =

㊷ 24 ÷ 8 =

㊸ 42 ÷ 7 =

㊹ 9 ÷ 9 =

㊺ 72 ÷ 8 =

Your Time

min.   sec.

Score

/45

Practice
Division from ÷6 to ÷9, ÷1

Target Time
2 / 3 / 4 min.
* Based on your time from the previous page, circle a target time for completing this page.

Date / /   **Name**

● **Divide.**

① 64 ÷ 8 =

② 2 ÷ 1 =

③ 27 ÷ 9 =

④ 36 ÷ 6 =

⑤ 28 ÷ 7 =

⑥ 8 ÷ 8 =

⑦ 48 ÷ 6 =

⑧ 63 ÷ 9 =

⑨ 9 ÷ 1 =

⑩ 42 ÷ 7 =

⑪ 32 ÷ 8 =

⑫ 12 ÷ 6 =

⑬ 35 ÷ 7 =

⑭ 3 ÷ 1 =

⑮ 81 ÷ 9 =

⑯ 24 ÷ 8 =

⑰ 8 ÷ 1 =

⑱ 6 ÷ 6 =

⑲ 36 ÷ 9 =

⑳ 63 ÷ 7 =

㉑ 48 ÷ 8 =

㉒ 18 ÷ 6 =

㉓ 18 ÷ 9 =

㉔ 5 ÷ 1 =

㉕ 14 ÷ 7 =

㉖ 56 ÷ 8 =

㉗ 24 ÷ 6 =

㉘ 1 ÷ 1 =

㉙ 45 ÷ 9 =

㉚ 49 ÷ 7 =

㉛ 72 ÷ 8 =

㉜ 30 ÷ 6 =

㉝ 4 ÷ 1 =

㉞ 9 ÷ 9 =

㉟ 56 ÷ 7 =

㊱ 16 ÷ 8 =

㊲ 7 ÷ 1 =

㊳ 54 ÷ 9 =

㊴ 54 ÷ 6 =

㊵ 21 ÷ 7 =

㊶ 40 ÷ 8 =

㊷ 72 ÷ 9 =

㊸ 7 ÷ 7 =

㊹ 6 ÷ 1 =

㊺ 42 ÷ 6 =

Your Time
min.   sec.

Score
/45

© Kumon Publishing Co., Ltd.

40

Practice
Division from ÷6 to ÷9, ÷1

Target Time

2 / 3 / 4 min.

* Based on your time from the previous page, circle a target time for completing this page.

Date   /   /

Name

● **Divide.**

(1) $45 \div 9 =$

(2) $64 \div 8 =$

(3) $1 \div 1 =$

(4) $24 \div 6 =$

(5) $42 \div 7 =$

(6) $56 \div 8 =$

(7) $18 \div 9 =$

(8) $8 \div 1 =$

(9) $63 \div 7 =$

(10) $6 \div 6 =$

(11) $24 \div 8 =$

(12) $81 \div 9 =$

(13) $21 \div 7 =$

(14) $30 \div 6 =$

(15) $2 \div 1 =$

(16) $9 \div 9 =$

(17) $28 \div 7 =$

(18) $42 \div 6 =$

(19) $3 \div 1 =$

(20) $16 \div 8 =$

(21) $54 \div 9 =$

(22) $35 \div 7 =$

(23) $48 \div 6 =$

(24) $4 \div 1 =$

(25) $72 \div 8 =$

(26) $72 \div 9 =$

(27) $12 \div 6 =$

(28) $7 \div 7 =$

(29) $7 \div 1 =$

(30) $40 \div 8 =$

(31) $8 \div 8 =$

(32) $27 \div 9 =$

(33) $14 \div 7 =$

(34) $6 \div 1 =$

(35) $36 \div 6 =$

(36) $56 \div 7 =$

(37) $63 \div 9 =$

(38) $32 \div 8 =$

(39) $5 \div 1 =$

(40) $54 \div 6 =$

(41) $48 \div 8 =$

(42) $36 \div 9 =$

(43) $49 \div 7 =$

(44) $18 \div 6 =$

(45) $9 \div 1 =$

Your Time

min.   sec.

Score

/45

Sprint
Division from ÷1 to ÷9

Date   Name

/   /

● **Divide. Time how long it takes to complete the division problems. Log your time below.**

① $14 \div 2 =$

② $40 \div 8 =$

③ $15 \div 5 =$

④ $4 \div 4 =$

⑤ $4 \div 1 =$

⑥ $27 \div 3 =$

⑦ $24 \div 6 =$

⑧ $64 \div 8 =$

⑨ $4 \div 2 =$

⑩ $35 \div 7 =$

⑪ $63 \div 9 =$

⑫ $18 \div 3 =$

⑬ $14 \div 7 =$

⑭ $40 \div 5 =$

⑮ $20 \div 4 =$

⑯ $9 \div 9 =$

⑰ $36 \div 6 =$

⑱ $2 \div 1 =$

⑲ $25 \div 5 =$

⑳ $8 \div 2 =$

㉑ $72 \div 9 =$

㉒ $63 \div 7 =$

㉓ $16 \div 8 =$

㉔ $24 \div 4 =$

㉕ $42 \div 6 =$

㉖ $9 \div 1 =$

㉗ $9 \div 3 =$

㉘ $5 \div 5 =$

㉙ $45 \div 9 =$

㉚ $18 \div 2 =$

㉛ $49 \div 7 =$

㉜ $6 \div 3 =$

㉝ $32 \div 8 =$

㉞ $6 \div 1 =$

㉟ $6 \div 6 =$

㊱ $81 \div 9 =$

㊲ $12 \div 4 =$

㊳ $8 \div 1 =$

㊴ $10 \div 2 =$

㊵ $48 \div 6 =$

㊶ $30 \div 5 =$

㊷ $28 \div 7 =$

㊸ $32 \div 4 =$

㊹ $21 \div 3 =$

㊺ $24 \div 8 =$

Review any incorrect answers and remember not to rush.

Score

Your Time

min.   sec.   /45

42

Sprint
Division from ÷1 to ÷9

Target Time

2 / 3 / 4 min.

* Based on your time from the previous page, circle a target time for completing this page.

Date   /   /

Name

● **Divide.**

① 12 ÷ 3 =

② 18 ÷ 9 =

③ 54 ÷ 6 =

④ 8 ÷ 8 =

⑤ 56 ÷ 7 =

⑥ 12 ÷ 4 =

⑦ 5 ÷ 1 =

⑧ 20 ÷ 5 =

⑨ 6 ÷ 2 =

⑩ 24 ÷ 3 =

⑪ 1 ÷ 1 =

⑫ 16 ÷ 2 =

⑬ 8 ÷ 4 =

⑭ 42 ÷ 7 =

⑮ 36 ÷ 9 =

⑯ 2 ÷ 2 =

⑰ 18 ÷ 6 =

⑱ 56 ÷ 8 =

⑲ 15 ÷ 3 =

⑳ 3 ÷ 1 =

㉑ 54 ÷ 9 =

㉒ 10 ÷ 5 =

㉓ 8 ÷ 2 =

㉔ 28 ÷ 4 =

㉕ 36 ÷ 6 =

㉖ 5 ÷ 5 =

㉗ 35 ÷ 7 =

㉘ 72 ÷ 8 =

㉙ 3 ÷ 3 =

㉚ 30 ÷ 6 =

㉛ 18 ÷ 9 =

㉜ 21 ÷ 7 =

㉝ 12 ÷ 2 =

㉞ 16 ÷ 4 =

㉟ 45 ÷ 5 =

㊱ 7 ÷ 1 =

㊲ 48 ÷ 8 =

㊳ 27 ÷ 9 =

㊴ 6 ÷ 3 =

㊵ 8 ÷ 1 =

㊶ 7 ÷ 7 =

㊷ 36 ÷ 4 =

㊸ 32 ÷ 8 =

㊹ 35 ÷ 5 =

㊺ 12 ÷ 6 =

Score

Your Time

min.   sec.   /45

Sprint
Division from ÷1 to ÷9

Target Time
2 / 3 / 4 min.
* Based on your time from the previous page, circle a target time for completing this page.

Date   /   /   Name

● **Divide.**

① 8 ÷ 4 =

② 56 ÷ 7 =

③ 18 ÷ 2 =

④ 40 ÷ 8 =

⑤ 5 ÷ 5 =

⑥ 9 ÷ 3 =

⑦ 24 ÷ 6 =

⑧ 72 ÷ 9 =

⑨ 4 ÷ 2 =

⑩ 32 ÷ 4 =

⑪ 12 ÷ 3 =

⑫ 49 ÷ 7 =

⑬ 12 ÷ 6 =

⑭ 5 ÷ 1 =

⑮ 56 ÷ 8 =

⑯ 28 ÷ 7 =

⑰ 45 ÷ 9 =

⑱ 15 ÷ 5 =

⑲ 72 ÷ 8 =

⑳ 1 ÷ 1 =

㉑ 30 ÷ 6 =

㉒ 27 ÷ 9 =

㉓ 24 ÷ 4 =

㉔ 16 ÷ 2 =

㉕ 7 ÷ 7 =

㉖ 21 ÷ 3 =

㉗ 16 ÷ 8 =

㉘ 10 ÷ 2 =

㉙ 20 ÷ 5 =

㉚ 7 ÷ 1 =

㉛ 54 ÷ 9 =

㉜ 12 ÷ 4 =

㉝ 54 ÷ 6 =

㉞ 15 ÷ 3 =

㉟ 2 ÷ 1 =

㊱ 30 ÷ 5 =

㊲ 2 ÷ 2 =

㊳ 24 ÷ 3 =

㊴ 21 ÷ 7 =

㊵ 32 ÷ 8 =

㊶ 6 ÷ 1 =

㊷ 42 ÷ 6 =

㊸ 36 ÷ 4 =

㊹ 9 ÷ 9 =

㊺ 40 ÷ 5 =

Your Time

min.   sec.

Score

/45

Sprint
Division from ÷1 to ÷9

Target Time

2 / 3 / 4 min.

* Based on your time from the previous page, circle a target time for completing this page.

Date / /   Name

● **Divide.**

① $45 \div 5 =$

② $3 \div 1 =$

③ $48 \div 8 =$

④ $27 \div 3 =$

⑤ $6 \div 6 =$

⑥ $8 \div 4 =$

⑦ $35 \div 7 =$

⑧ $6 \div 2 =$

⑨ $36 \div 9 =$

⑩ $10 \div 5 =$

⑪ $18 \div 3 =$

⑫ $9 \div 1 =$

⑬ $48 \div 6 =$

⑭ $28 \div 4 =$

⑮ $24 \div 8 =$

⑯ $7 \div 7 =$

⑰ $63 \div 9 =$

⑱ $8 \div 2 =$

⑲ $25 \div 5 =$

⑳ $8 \div 1 =$

㉑ $42 \div 7 =$

㉒ $6 \div 3 =$

㉓ $32 \div 8 =$

㉔ $4 \div 4 =$

㉕ $18 \div 6 =$

㉖ $81 \div 9 =$

㉗ $12 \div 2 =$

㉘ $35 \div 5 =$

㉙ $14 \div 7 =$

㉚ $4 \div 1 =$

㉛ $54 \div 9 =$

㉜ $3 \div 3 =$

㉝ $24 \div 6 =$

㉞ $20 \div 4 =$

㉟ $64 \div 8 =$

㊱ $14 \div 2 =$

㊲ $15 \div 5 =$

㊳ $18 \div 9 =$

㊴ $5 \div 1 =$

㊵ $16 \div 2 =$

㊶ $36 \div 6 =$

㊷ $16 \div 4 =$

㊸ $8 \div 8 =$

㊹ $63 \div 7 =$

㊺ $21 \div 3 =$

Your Time

min.   sec.

Score

/45

Sprint
Division from ÷1 to ÷9

Target Time

2 / 3 / 4 min.

* Based on your time from the previous page, circle a target time for completing this page.

Date   **Name**

/   /

● **Divide.**

① 30 ÷ 6 =

② 9 ÷ 1 =

③ 12 ÷ 3 =

④ 8 ÷ 8 =

⑤ 15 ÷ 5 =

⑥ 49 ÷ 7 =

⑦ 16 ÷ 2 =

⑧ 12 ÷ 6 =

⑨ 20 ÷ 4 =

⑩ 35 ÷ 5 =

⑪ 3 ÷ 3 =

⑫ 72 ÷ 8 =

⑬ 28 ÷ 7 =

⑭ 63 ÷ 9 =

⑮ 5 ÷ 5 =

⑯ 18 ÷ 2 =

⑰ 32 ÷ 8 =

⑱ 54 ÷ 9 =

⑲ 12 ÷ 4 =

⑳ 48 ÷ 6 =

㉑ 2 ÷ 1 =

㉒ 15 ÷ 3 =

㉓ 7 ÷ 7 =

㉔ 12 ÷ 2 =

㉕ 5 ÷ 1 =

㉖ 45 ÷ 5 =

㉗ 36 ÷ 9 =

㉘ 56 ÷ 8 =

㉙ 8 ÷ 4 =

㉚ 18 ÷ 6 =

㉛ 7 ÷ 1 =

㉜ 42 ÷ 7 =

㉝ 8 ÷ 2 =

㉞ 27 ÷ 9 =

㉟ 6 ÷ 3 =

㊱ 32 ÷ 4 =

㊲ 36 ÷ 6 =

㊳ 4 ÷ 1 =

㊴ 25 ÷ 5 =

㊵ 21 ÷ 7 =

㊶ 36 ÷ 4 =

㊷ 9 ÷ 9 =

㊸ 21 ÷ 3 =

㊹ 40 ÷ 8 =

㊺ 4 ÷ 2 =

Score

Your Time

min.   sec.   /45

Sprint
Division from ÷1 to ÷9

Target Time

2 / 3 / 4 min.

* Based on your time from the previous page,
circle a target time for completing this page.

Date   /   /

Name

● **Divide.**

① $56 \div 7 =$

② $9 \div 3 =$

③ $16 \div 8 =$

④ $40 \div 5 =$

⑤ $36 \div 9 =$

⑥ $28 \div 4 =$

⑦ $54 \div 6 =$

⑧ $2 \div 2 =$

⑨ $24 \div 6 =$

⑩ $35 \div 7 =$

⑪ $10 \div 5 =$

⑫ $8 \div 1 =$

⑬ $24 \div 8 =$

⑭ $18 \div 3 =$

⑮ $81 \div 9 =$

⑯ $6 \div 3 =$

⑰ $1 \div 1 =$

⑱ $10 \div 2 =$

⑲ $12 \div 4 =$

⑳ $48 \div 8 =$

㉑ $14 \div 7 =$

㉒ $30 \div 6 =$

㉓ $4 \div 4 =$

㉔ $72 \div 9 =$

㉕ $20 \div 5 =$

㉖ $27 \div 3 =$

㉗ $3 \div 1 =$

㉘ $14 \div 2 =$

㉙ $32 \div 8 =$

㉚ $25 \div 5 =$

㉛ $63 \div 7 =$

㉜ $24 \div 3 =$

㉝ $45 \div 9 =$

㉞ $6 \div 1 =$

㉟ $6 \div 6 =$

㊱ $16 \div 4 =$

㊲ $6 \div 2 =$

㊳ $42 \div 6 =$

㊴ $7 \div 7 =$

㊵ $64 \div 8 =$

㊶ $30 \div 5 =$

㊷ $8 \div 2 =$

㊸ $18 \div 9 =$

㊹ $9 \div 1 =$

㊺ $24 \div 4 =$

Score

Your Time

min.   sec.   /45

47 Sprint Division from ÷1 to ÷9

Target Time
2 / 3 / 4 min.
* Based on your time from the previous page, circle a target time for completing this page.

Date / / Name

● **Divide.**

① 48 ÷ 8 =
② 10 ÷ 2 =
③ 16 ÷ 4 =
④ 8 ÷ 1 =
⑤ 6 ÷ 6 =
⑥ 18 ÷ 9 =
⑦ 27 ÷ 3 =
⑧ 35 ÷ 7 =
⑨ 20 ÷ 5 =
⑩ 8 ÷ 8 =
⑪ 8 ÷ 4 =
⑫ 14 ÷ 2 =
⑬ 3 ÷ 1 =
⑭ 36 ÷ 6 =
⑮ 36 ÷ 9 =
⑯ 40 ÷ 5 =
⑰ 9 ÷ 3 =
⑱ 28 ÷ 4 =
⑲ 40 ÷ 8 =
⑳ 16 ÷ 2 =
㉑ 42 ÷ 7 =
㉒ 10 ÷ 5 =
㉓ 1 ÷ 1 =
㉔ 54 ÷ 6 =
㉕ 18 ÷ 3 =
㉖ 45 ÷ 9 =
㉗ 49 ÷ 7 =
㉘ 72 ÷ 8 =
㉙ 32 ÷ 4 =
㉚ 4 ÷ 2 =
㉛ 18 ÷ 6 =
㉜ 4 ÷ 1 =
㉝ 63 ÷ 9 =
㉞ 30 ÷ 5 =
㉟ 24 ÷ 3 =
㊱ 7 ÷ 7 =
㊲ 24 ÷ 8 =
㊳ 20 ÷ 4 =
㊴ 45 ÷ 5 =
㊵ 8 ÷ 2 =
㊶ 6 ÷ 1 =
㊷ 3 ÷ 3 =
㊸ 12 ÷ 6 =
㊹ 72 ÷ 9 =
㊺ 63 ÷ 7 =

Your Time min. sec.

Score /45

48
Sprint
Division from ÷1 to ÷9

Target Time
2 / 3 / 4 min.
* Based on your time from the previous page, circle a target time for completing this page.

Date   /   /   Name

● **Divide.**

① 27 ÷ 9 =

② 56 ÷ 8 =

③ 36 ÷ 4 =

④ 10 ÷ 5 =

⑤ 10 ÷ 2 =

⑥ 12 ÷ 3 =

⑦ 48 ÷ 6 =

⑧ 5 ÷ 1 =

⑨ 14 ÷ 7 =

⑩ 64 ÷ 8 =

⑪ 9 ÷ 9 =

⑫ 21 ÷ 3 =

⑬ 24 ÷ 6 =

⑭ 18 ÷ 2 =

⑮ 8 ÷ 4 =

⑯ 18 ÷ 6 =

⑰ 9 ÷ 1 =

⑱ 5 ÷ 5 =

⑲ 12 ÷ 2 =

⑳ 6 ÷ 3 =

㉑ 30 ÷ 6 =

㉒ 56 ÷ 7 =

㉓ 36 ÷ 9 =

㉔ 72 ÷ 8 =

㉕ 2 ÷ 2 =

㉖ 24 ÷ 4 =

㉗ 14 ÷ 7 =

㉘ 7 ÷ 1 =

㉙ 15 ÷ 5 =

㉚ 18 ÷ 3 =

㉛ 12 ÷ 4 =

㉜ 28 ÷ 7 =

㉝ 54 ÷ 9 =

㉞ 16 ÷ 8 =

㉟ 25 ÷ 5 =

㊱ 6 ÷ 2 =

㊲ 8 ÷ 1 =

㊳ 4 ÷ 4 =

㊴ 42 ÷ 6 =

㊵ 15 ÷ 3 =

㊶ 32 ÷ 8 =

㊷ 81 ÷ 9 =

㊸ 21 ÷ 7 =

㊹ 2 ÷ 1 =

㊺ 35 ÷ 5 =

Your Time

min.   sec.

Score

/45

49

Sprint
Division from ÷1 to ÷9

Target Time
2 / 3 / 4 min.
* Based on your time from the previous page,
circle a target time for completing this page.

Date
/   /

Name

● **Divide.**

① 7 ÷ 1 =

② 30 ÷ 6 =

③ 45 ÷ 5 =

④ 8 ÷ 4 =

⑤ 18 ÷ 3 =

⑥ 7 ÷ 7 =

⑦ 72 ÷ 8 =

⑧ 6 ÷ 2 =

⑨ 12 ÷ 6 =

⑩ 32 ÷ 4 =

⑪ 5 ÷ 5 =

⑫ 9 ÷ 1 =

⑬ 12 ÷ 3 =

⑭ 63 ÷ 9 =

⑮ 35 ÷ 7 =

⑯ 64 ÷ 8 =

⑰ 54 ÷ 6 =

⑱ 4 ÷ 2 =

⑲ 54 ÷ 9 =

⑳ 21 ÷ 7 =

㉑ 16 ÷ 4 =

㉒ 42 ÷ 6 =

㉓ 1 ÷ 1 =

㉔ 30 ÷ 5 =

㉕ 16 ÷ 8 =

㉖ 56 ÷ 7 =

㉗ 9 ÷ 3 =

㉘ 36 ÷ 4 =

㉙ 10 ÷ 2 =

㉚ 9 ÷ 9 =

㉛ 24 ÷ 3 =

㉜ 20 ÷ 5 =

㉝ 56 ÷ 8 =

㉞ 6 ÷ 1 =

㉟ 18 ÷ 9 =

㊱ 63 ÷ 7 =

㊲ 14 ÷ 2 =

㊳ 24 ÷ 6 =

㊴ 3 ÷ 3 =

㊵ 40 ÷ 8 =

㊶ 24 ÷ 4 =

㊷ 81 ÷ 9 =

㊸ 3 ÷ 1 =

㊹ 16 ÷ 2 =

㊺ 25 ÷ 5 =

Your Time

min.   sec.

Score

/45

50

Sprint
Division from ÷1 to ÷9

Target Time
2 / 3 / 4 min.
* Based on your time from the previous page, circle a target time for completing this page.

Date
/   /

Name

● **Divide.**

① $2 \div 2 =$

② $36 \div 6 =$

③ $4 \div 1 =$

④ $10 \div 5 =$

⑤ $24 \div 8 =$

⑥ $15 \div 3 =$

⑦ $72 \div 9 =$

⑧ $14 \div 7 =$

⑨ $5 \div 1 =$

⑩ $12 \div 2 =$

⑪ $32 \div 8 =$

⑫ $40 \div 5 =$

⑬ $18 \div 6 =$

⑭ $4 \div 4 =$

⑮ $36 \div 9 =$

⑯ $2 \div 1 =$

⑰ $49 \div 7 =$

⑱ $48 \div 8 =$

⑲ $8 \div 2 =$

⑳ $45 \div 9 =$

㉑ $12 \div 4 =$

㉒ $30 \div 5 =$

㉓ $21 \div 3 =$

㉔ $2 \div 1 =$

㉕ $48 \div 6 =$

㉖ $20 \div 4 =$

㉗ $8 \div 8 =$

㉘ $18 \div 2 =$

㉙ $6 \div 3 =$

㉚ $42 \div 7 =$

㉛ $27 \div 9 =$

㉜ $35 \div 5 =$

㉝ $16 \div 4 =$

㉞ $8 \div 1 =$

㉟ $6 \div 6 =$

㊱ $27 \div 3 =$

㊲ $28 \div 7 =$

㊳ $10 \div 2 =$

㊴ $72 \div 8 =$

㊵ $54 \div 9 =$

㊶ $28 \div 4 =$

㊷ $12 \div 6 =$

㊸ $3 \div 3 =$

㊹ $35 \div 7 =$

㊺ $15 \div 5 =$

Your Time

Score

min.   sec.   /45

Sprint
Division from ÷1 to ÷9

Target Time
2 / 3 / 4 min.
* Based on your time from the previous page, circle a target time for completing this page.

Date / /　**Name**

● **Divide.**

① 24 ÷ 3 =

② 32 ÷ 8 =

③ 15 ÷ 5 =

④ 12 ÷ 6 =

⑤ 49 ÷ 7 =

⑥ 27 ÷ 9 =

⑦ 20 ÷ 4 =

⑧ 1 ÷ 1 =

⑨ 8 ÷ 2 =

⑩ 6 ÷ 3 =

⑪ 56 ÷ 8 =

⑫ 18 ÷ 6 =

⑬ 24 ÷ 4 =

⑭ 35 ÷ 7 =

⑮ 4 ÷ 1 =

⑯ 45 ÷ 9 =

⑰ 40 ÷ 5 =

⑱ 2 ÷ 2 =

⑲ 12 ÷ 4 =

⑳ 8 ÷ 1 =

㉑ 14 ÷ 7 =

㉒ 12 ÷ 3 =

㉓ 12 ÷ 2 =

㉔ 64 ÷ 8 =

㉕ 5 ÷ 5 =

㉖ 2 ÷ 1 =

㉗ 54 ÷ 9 =

㉘ 54 ÷ 6 =

㉙ 28 ÷ 7 =

㉚ 15 ÷ 3 =

㉛ 14 ÷ 2 =

㉜ 30 ÷ 6 =

㉝ 63 ÷ 7 =

㉞ 4 ÷ 4 =

㉟ 72 ÷ 9 =

㊱ 16 ÷ 8 =

㊲ 27 ÷ 3 =

㊳ 6 ÷ 1 =

㊴ 9 ÷ 9 =

㊵ 25 ÷ 5 =

㊶ 4 ÷ 2 =

㊷ 42 ÷ 6 =

㊸ 32 ÷ 4 =

㊹ 24 ÷ 8 =

㊺ 45 ÷ 5 =

Your Time

min.　sec.

Score

/45

52
Sprint
Division from ÷1 to ÷9

Target Time
2 / 3 / 4 min.
* Based on your time from the previous page, circle a target time for completing this page.

Date / /

Name

● Divide.

① $16 \div 4 =$

② $63 \div 9 =$

③ $72 \div 8 =$

④ $42 \div 7 =$

⑤ $9 \div 3 =$

⑥ $10 \div 5 =$

⑦ $18 \div 2 =$

⑧ $3 \div 1 =$

⑨ $36 \div 6 =$

⑩ $81 \div 9 =$

⑪ $16 \div 8 =$

⑫ $28 \div 4 =$

⑬ $12 \div 3 =$

⑭ $56 \div 7 =$

⑮ $6 \div 2 =$

⑯ $18 \div 9 =$

⑰ $48 \div 6 =$

⑱ $40 \div 8 =$

⑲ $30 \div 5 =$

⑳ $7 \div 1 =$

㉑ $28 \div 7 =$

㉒ $3 \div 3 =$

㉓ $72 \div 9 =$

㉔ $8 \div 4 =$

㉕ $18 \div 6 =$

㉖ $10 \div 2 =$

㉗ $48 \div 8 =$

㉘ $9 \div 1 =$

㉙ $35 \div 5 =$

㉚ $7 \div 7 =$

㉛ $24 \div 6 =$

㉜ $18 \div 3 =$

㉝ $36 \div 4 =$

㉞ $16 \div 2 =$

㉟ $21 \div 7 =$

㊱ $20 \div 5 =$

㊲ $5 \div 1 =$

㊳ $8 \div 8 =$

㊴ $21 \div 3 =$

㊵ $36 \div 9 =$

㊶ $4 \div 2 =$

㊷ $6 \div 6 =$

㊸ $20 \div 4 =$

㊹ $40 \div 5 =$

㊺ $6 \div 1 =$

Score

Your Time

min.   sec.

/45

Sprint
Division from ÷1 to ÷9

Target Time
2 / 3 / 4 min.
* Based on your time from the previous page, circle a target time for completing this page.

Date
/   /

Name

● **Divide.**

① $10 \div 5 =$

② $6 \div 2 =$

③ $56 \div 8 =$

④ $16 \div 4 =$

⑤ $54 \div 9 =$

⑥ $8 \div 1 =$

⑦ $7 \div 7 =$

⑧ $27 \div 3 =$

⑨ $10 \div 2 =$

⑩ $35 \div 5 =$

⑪ $8 \div 4 =$

⑫ $18 \div 6 =$

⑬ $64 \div 8 =$

⑭ $63 \div 7 =$

⑮ $63 \div 9 =$

⑯ $24 \div 6 =$

⑰ $3 \div 3 =$

⑱ $2 \div 1 =$

⑲ $25 \div 5 =$

⑳ $18 \div 2 =$

㉑ $21 \div 7 =$

㉒ $4 \div 4 =$

㉓ $18 \div 9 =$

㉔ $48 \div 8 =$

㉕ $12 \div 3 =$

㉖ $36 \div 4 =$

㉗ $6 \div 6 =$

㉘ $4 \div 1 =$

㉙ $12 \div 2 =$

㉚ $40 \div 5 =$

㉛ $9 \div 3 =$

㉜ $49 \div 7 =$

㉝ $6 \div 1 =$

㉞ $16 \div 8 =$

㉟ $48 \div 6 =$

㊱ $45 \div 9 =$

㊲ $24 \div 4 =$

㊳ $20 \div 5 =$

㊴ $2 \div 2 =$

㊵ $6 \div 3 =$

㊶ $35 \div 7 =$

㊷ $7 \div 1 =$

㊸ $27 \div 9 =$

㊹ $36 \div 6 =$

㊺ $32 \div 8 =$

Your Time

min.   sec.

Score

/45

Sprint
Division from ÷1 to ÷9

Target Time

2 / **3** / **4** min.

* Based on your time from the previous page, circle a target time for completing this page.

Date   /   /   Name

● **Divide.**

① $54 \div 6 =$

② $5 \div 1 =$

③ $12 \div 3 =$

④ $14 \div 7 =$

⑤ $14 \div 2 =$

⑥ $12 \div 4 =$

⑦ $81 \div 9 =$

⑧ $8 \div 8 =$

⑨ $15 \div 5 =$

⑩ $30 \div 6 =$

⑪ $21 \div 3 =$

⑫ $6 \div 1 =$

⑬ $28 \div 7 =$

⑭ $6 \div 2 =$

⑮ $64 \div 8 =$

⑯ $9 \div 1 =$

⑰ $32 \div 4 =$

⑱ $35 \div 7 =$

⑲ $9 \div 9 =$

⑳ $24 \div 3 =$

㉑ $12 \div 6 =$

㉒ $30 \div 5 =$

㉓ $8 \div 2 =$

㉔ $40 \div 8 =$

㉕ $4 \div 4 =$

㉖ $56 \div 7 =$

㉗ $27 \div 9 =$

㉘ $18 \div 3 =$

㉙ $1 \div 1 =$

㉚ $42 \div 6 =$

㉛ $16 \div 2 =$

㉜ $36 \div 9 =$

㉝ $72 \div 8 =$

㉞ $20 \div 4 =$

㉟ $42 \div 7 =$

㊱ $10 \div 5 =$

㊲ $3 \div 1 =$

㊳ $6 \div 6 =$

㊴ $28 \div 4 =$

㊵ $15 \div 3 =$

㊶ $5 \div 5 =$

㊷ $72 \div 9 =$

㊸ $24 \div 8 =$

㊹ $45 \div 5 =$

㊺ $4 \div 2 =$

Your Time

min.   sec.

Score

/45

Sprint
Division from ÷1 to ÷9

Target Time

2 / 3 / 4 min.

* Based on your time from the previous page, circle a target time for completing this page.

Date / / **Name**

● **Divide.**

① 42 ÷ 7 =

② 8 ÷ 2 =

③ 9 ÷ 1 =

④ 10 ÷ 5 =

⑤ 63 ÷ 9 =

⑥ 15 ÷ 3 =

⑦ 8 ÷ 8 =

⑧ 56 ÷ 7 =

⑨ 18 ÷ 6 =

⑩ 32 ÷ 4 =

⑪ 14 ÷ 2 =

⑫ 2 ÷ 1 =

⑬ 54 ÷ 9 =

⑭ 20 ÷ 5 =

⑮ 27 ÷ 3 =

⑯ 4 ÷ 4 =

⑰ 64 ÷ 8 =

⑱ 30 ÷ 6 =

⑲ 14 ÷ 7 =

⑳ 18 ÷ 2 =

㉑ 9 ÷ 3 =

㉒ 7 ÷ 1 =

㉓ 9 ÷ 9 =

㉔ 40 ÷ 5 =

㉕ 48 ÷ 8 =

㉖ 12 ÷ 4 =

㉗ 4 ÷ 2 =

㉘ 28 ÷ 7 =

㉙ 6 ÷ 6 =

㉚ 30 ÷ 5 =

㉛ 6 ÷ 3 =

㉜ 3 ÷ 1 =

㉝ 40 ÷ 8 =

㉞ 35 ÷ 5 =

㉟ 48 ÷ 6 =

㊱ 36 ÷ 9 =

㊲ 20 ÷ 4 =

㊳ 63 ÷ 7 =

㊴ 2 ÷ 2 =

㊵ 24 ÷ 3 =

㊶ 24 ÷ 8 =

㊷ 36 ÷ 6 =

㊸ 72 ÷ 9 =

㊹ 28 ÷ 4 =

㊺ 5 ÷ 1 =

Your Time

min.   sec.

Score

/45

Sprint
Division from ÷1 to ÷9

Target Time

2 / **3** / **4** min.

* Based on your time from the previous page, circle a target time for completing this page.

Date   Name

/   /

● **Divide.**

① $24 \div 8 =$

② $25 \div 5 =$

③ $6 \div 1 =$

④ $12 \div 3 =$

⑤ $42 \div 6 =$

⑥ $9 \div 9 =$

⑦ $16 \div 2 =$

⑧ $8 \div 4 =$

⑨ $42 \div 7 =$

⑩ $56 \div 8 =$

⑪ $15 \div 5 =$

⑫ $24 \div 6 =$

⑬ $10 \div 2 =$

⑭ $6 \div 3 =$

⑮ $81 \div 9 =$

⑯ $16 \div 4 =$

⑰ $8 \div 1 =$

⑱ $7 \div 7 =$

⑲ $16 \div 8 =$

⑳ $36 \div 4 =$

㉑ $12 \div 2 =$

㉒ $3 \div 3 =$

㉓ $27 \div 9 =$

㉔ $20 \div 5 =$

㉕ $35 \div 7 =$

㉖ $7 \div 1 =$

㉗ $12 \div 6 =$

㉘ $72 \div 8 =$

㉙ $24 \div 4 =$

㉚ $1 \div 1 =$

㉛ $21 \div 7 =$

㉜ $45 \div 9 =$

㉝ $21 \div 3 =$

㉞ $6 \div 2 =$

㉟ $45 \div 5 =$

㊱ $48 \div 6 =$

㊲ $32 \div 8 =$

㊳ $18 \div 2 =$

㊴ $20 \div 4 =$

㊵ $18 \div 3 =$

㊶ $18 \div 9 =$

㊷ $49 \div 7 =$

㊸ $4 \div 1 =$

㊹ $54 \div 6 =$

㊺ $5 \div 5 =$

Congratulations!
You have really improved
your speed and accuracy!

Your Time

Score

min.   sec.   /45

Answer Key
Division

---

1 — Warm-Up: Division ÷2

1 Read each number sentence aloud. Trace each answer.

2 ÷ 2 = 1	8 ÷ 2 = 4	14 ÷ 2 = 7
4 ÷ 2 = 2	10 ÷ 2 = 5	16 ÷ 2 = 8
6 ÷ 2 = 3	12 ÷ 2 = 6	18 ÷ 2 = 9

2 Divide. Time how long it takes to complete the division problems. Log your time below.

2 ÷ 2 = 1	6 ÷ 2 = 3	18 ÷ 2 = 9
4 ÷ 2 = 2	10 ÷ 2 = 5	6 ÷ 2 = 3
6 ÷ 2 = 3	14 ÷ 2 = 7	12 ÷ 2 = 6
8 ÷ 2 = 4	18 ÷ 2 = 9	16 ÷ 2 = 8
10 ÷ 2 = 5	4 ÷ 2 = 2	10 ÷ 2 = 5
12 ÷ 2 = 6	8 ÷ 2 = 4	4 ÷ 2 = 2
14 ÷ 2 = 7	12 ÷ 2 = 6	2 ÷ 2 = 1
16 ÷ 2 = 8	16 ÷ 2 = 8	2 ÷ 2 = 1
18 ÷ 2 = 9	10 ÷ 2 = 5	14 ÷ 2 = 7
2 ÷ 2 = 1	14 ÷ 2 = 7	8 ÷ 2 = 4

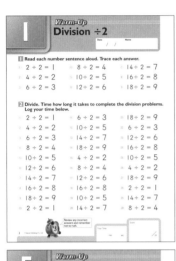

---

2 — Warm-Up: Division ÷3

1 Read each number sentence aloud. Trace each answer.

3 ÷ 3 = 1	12 ÷ 3 = 4	21 ÷ 3 = 7
6 ÷ 3 = 2	15 ÷ 3 = 5	24 ÷ 3 = 8
9 ÷ 3 = 3	18 ÷ 3 = 6	27 ÷ 3 = 9

2 Divide. Time how long it takes to complete the division problems. Log your time below.

3 ÷ 3 = 1	12 ÷ 3 = 4	21 ÷ 3 = 7
6 ÷ 3 = 2	18 ÷ 3 = 6	3 ÷ 3 = 1
9 ÷ 3 = 3	24 ÷ 3 = 8	18 ÷ 3 = 6
12 ÷ 3 = 4	3 ÷ 3 = 1	18 ÷ 3 = 6
15 ÷ 3 = 5	9 ÷ 3 = 3	12 ÷ 3 = 4
18 ÷ 3 = 6	15 ÷ 3 = 5	27 ÷ 3 = 9
21 ÷ 3 = 7	21 ÷ 3 = 7	6 ÷ 3 = 2
24 ÷ 3 = 8	27 ÷ 3 = 9	15 ÷ 3 = 5
27 ÷ 3 = 9	6 ÷ 3 = 2	9 ÷ 3 = 3
6 ÷ 3 = 2	9 ÷ 3 = 3	24 ÷ 3 = 8

---

3 — Warm-Up: Division ÷4

1 Read each number sentence aloud. Trace each answer.

4 ÷ 4 = 1	16 ÷ 4 = 4	28 ÷ 4 = 7
8 ÷ 4 = 2	20 ÷ 4 = 5	32 ÷ 4 = 8
12 ÷ 4 = 3	24 ÷ 4 = 6	36 ÷ 4 = 9

2 Divide. Time how long it takes to complete the division problems. Log your time below.

4 ÷ 4 = 1	12 ÷ 4 = 3	8 ÷ 4 = 2
8 ÷ 4 = 2	20 ÷ 4 = 5	16 ÷ 4 = 4
12 ÷ 4 = 3	28 ÷ 4 = 7	24 ÷ 4 = 6
16 ÷ 4 = 4	36 ÷ 4 = 9	32 ÷ 4 = 8
20 ÷ 4 = 5	8 ÷ 4 = 2	36 ÷ 4 = 9
24 ÷ 4 = 6	16 ÷ 4 = 4	12 ÷ 4 = 3
28 ÷ 4 = 7	24 ÷ 4 = 6	28 ÷ 4 = 7
32 ÷ 4 = 8	32 ÷ 4 = 8	4 ÷ 4 = 1
36 ÷ 4 = 9	4 ÷ 4 = 1	24 ÷ 4 = 6
4 ÷ 4 = 1	20 ÷ 4 = 5	16 ÷ 4 = 4

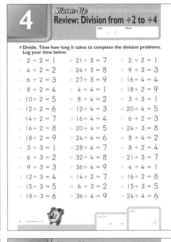

---

4 — Warm-Up: Review: Division from ÷2 to ÷4

● Divide. Time how long it takes to complete the division problems. Log your time below.

2 ÷ 2 = 1	21 ÷ 3 = 7	2 ÷ 2 = 1
4 ÷ 2 = 2	24 ÷ 3 = 8	9 ÷ 3 = 3
6 ÷ 2 = 3	27 ÷ 3 = 9	16 ÷ 4 = 4
8 ÷ 2 = 4	4 ÷ 4 = 1	18 ÷ 2 = 9
10 ÷ 2 = 5	8 ÷ 4 = 2	3 ÷ 3 = 1
12 ÷ 2 = 6	12 ÷ 4 = 3	20 ÷ 4 = 5
14 ÷ 2 = 7	16 ÷ 4 = 4	6 ÷ 2 = 3
16 ÷ 2 = 8	20 ÷ 4 = 5	24 ÷ 3 = 8
18 ÷ 2 = 9	24 ÷ 4 = 6	8 ÷ 4 = 2
3 ÷ 3 = 1	28 ÷ 4 = 7	8 ÷ 2 = 4
6 ÷ 3 = 2	32 ÷ 4 = 8	21 ÷ 3 = 7
9 ÷ 3 = 3	36 ÷ 4 = 9	4 ÷ 4 = 1
12 ÷ 3 = 4	14 ÷ 2 = 7	16 ÷ 2 = 8
15 ÷ 3 = 5	6 ÷ 3 = 2	15 ÷ 3 = 5
18 ÷ 3 = 6	36 ÷ 4 = 9	24 ÷ 4 = 6

---

5 — Warm-Up: Division ÷5

1 Read each number sentence aloud. Trace each answer.

5 ÷ 5 = 1	20 ÷ 5 = 4	35 ÷ 5 = 7
10 ÷ 5 = 2	25 ÷ 5 = 5	40 ÷ 5 = 8
15 ÷ 5 = 3	30 ÷ 5 = 6	45 ÷ 5 = 9

2 Divide. Time how long it takes to complete the division problems. Log your time below.

5 ÷ 5 = 1	20 ÷ 5 = 4	5 ÷ 5 = 1
10 ÷ 5 = 2	30 ÷ 5 = 6	40 ÷ 5 = 8
15 ÷ 5 = 3	40 ÷ 5 = 8	20 ÷ 5 = 4
20 ÷ 5 = 4	5 ÷ 5 = 1	30 ÷ 5 = 6
25 ÷ 5 = 5	15 ÷ 5 = 3	35 ÷ 5 = 7
30 ÷ 5 = 6	25 ÷ 5 = 5	10 ÷ 5 = 2
35 ÷ 5 = 7	35 ÷ 5 = 7	25 ÷ 5 = 5
40 ÷ 5 = 8	45 ÷ 5 = 9	45 ÷ 5 = 9
45 ÷ 5 = 9	10 ÷ 5 = 2	15 ÷ 5 = 3
10 ÷ 5 = 2	25 ÷ 5 = 5	30 ÷ 5 = 6

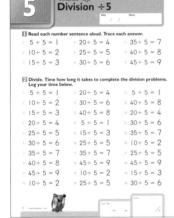

---

6 — Warm-Up: Division ÷6

1 Read each number sentence aloud. Trace each answer.

6 ÷ 6 = 1	24 ÷ 6 = 4	42 ÷ 6 = 7
12 ÷ 6 = 2	30 ÷ 6 = 5	48 ÷ 6 = 8
18 ÷ 6 = 3	36 ÷ 6 = 6	54 ÷ 6 = 9

2 Divide. Time how long it takes to complete the division problems. Log your time below.

6 ÷ 6 = 1	18 ÷ 6 = 3	54 ÷ 6 = 9
12 ÷ 6 = 2	30 ÷ 6 = 5	12 ÷ 6 = 2
18 ÷ 6 = 3	42 ÷ 6 = 7	24 ÷ 6 = 4
24 ÷ 6 = 4	54 ÷ 6 = 9	42 ÷ 6 = 7
30 ÷ 6 = 5	12 ÷ 6 = 2	18 ÷ 6 = 3
36 ÷ 6 = 6	24 ÷ 6 = 4	14 ÷ 7 = 2
42 ÷ 6 = 7	36 ÷ 6 = 6	48 ÷ 6 = 8
48 ÷ 6 = 8	48 ÷ 6 = 8	6 ÷ 6 = 1
54 ÷ 6 = 9	18 ÷ 6 = 3	36 ÷ 6 = 6
6 ÷ 6 = 1	6 ÷ 6 = 1	54 ÷ 6 = 9

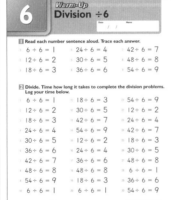

---

7 — Warm-Up: Division ÷7

1 Read each number sentence aloud. Trace each answer.

7 ÷ 7 = 1	28 ÷ 7 = 4	49 ÷ 7 = 7
14 ÷ 7 = 2	35 ÷ 7 = 5	56 ÷ 7 = 8
21 ÷ 7 = 3	42 ÷ 7 = 6	63 ÷ 7 = 9

2 Divide. Time how long it takes to complete the division problems. Log your time below.

7 ÷ 7 = 1	28 ÷ 7 = 4	63 ÷ 7 = 9
14 ÷ 7 = 2	42 ÷ 7 = 6	21 ÷ 7 = 3
21 ÷ 7 = 3	56 ÷ 7 = 8	7 ÷ 7 = 1
28 ÷ 7 = 4	7 ÷ 7 = 1	49 ÷ 7 = 7
35 ÷ 7 = 5	21 ÷ 7 = 3	42 ÷ 7 = 6
42 ÷ 7 = 6	35 ÷ 7 = 5	14 ÷ 7 = 2
49 ÷ 7 = 7	49 ÷ 7 = 7	35 ÷ 7 = 5
56 ÷ 7 = 8	63 ÷ 7 = 9	56 ÷ 7 = 8
63 ÷ 7 = 9	56 ÷ 7 = 8	28 ÷ 7 = 4
14 ÷ 7 = 2	28 ÷ 7 = 4	49 ÷ 7 = 7

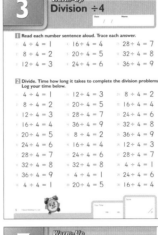

---

8 — Warm-Up: Review: Division from ÷5 to ÷7

● Divide. Time how long it takes to complete the division problems. Log your time below.

5 ÷ 5 = 1	42 ÷ 6 = 7	20 ÷ 5 = 4
10 ÷ 5 = 2	48 ÷ 6 = 8	30 ÷ 6 = 5
15 ÷ 5 = 3	54 ÷ 6 = 9	21 ÷ 7 = 3
20 ÷ 5 = 4	7 ÷ 7 = 1	35 ÷ 7 = 5
25 ÷ 5 = 5	14 ÷ 7 = 2	12 ÷ 6 = 2
30 ÷ 5 = 6	21 ÷ 7 = 3	56 ÷ 7 = 8
35 ÷ 5 = 7	28 ÷ 7 = 4	15 ÷ 5 = 3
40 ÷ 5 = 8	35 ÷ 7 = 5	36 ÷ 6 = 6
45 ÷ 5 = 9	42 ÷ 7 = 6	14 ÷ 7 = 2
6 ÷ 6 = 1	49 ÷ 7 = 7	40 ÷ 5 = 8
12 ÷ 6 = 2	56 ÷ 7 = 8	42 ÷ 6 = 7
18 ÷ 6 = 3	63 ÷ 7 = 9	28 ÷ 7 = 4
24 ÷ 6 = 4	25 ÷ 5 = 5	5 ÷ 5 = 1
30 ÷ 6 = 5	6 ÷ 6 = 1	54 ÷ 6 = 9
36 ÷ 6 = 6	63 ÷ 7 = 9	42 ÷ 7 = 6

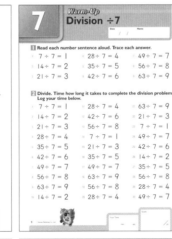

---

9 — Warm-Up: Division ÷8

1 Read each number sentence aloud. Trace each answer.

8 ÷ 8 = 1	32 ÷ 8 = 4	56 ÷ 8 = 7
16 ÷ 8 = 2	40 ÷ 8 = 5	64 ÷ 8 = 8
24 ÷ 8 = 3	48 ÷ 8 = 6	72 ÷ 8 = 9

2 Divide. Time how long it takes to complete the division problems. Log your time below.

8 ÷ 8 = 1	24 ÷ 8 = 3	16 ÷ 8 = 2
16 ÷ 8 = 2	40 ÷ 8 = 5	32 ÷ 8 = 4
24 ÷ 8 = 3	56 ÷ 8 = 7	72 ÷ 8 = 9
32 ÷ 8 = 4	72 ÷ 8 = 9	24 ÷ 8 = 3
40 ÷ 8 = 5	16 ÷ 8 = 2	40 ÷ 8 = 5
48 ÷ 8 = 6	32 ÷ 8 = 4	48 ÷ 8 = 6
56 ÷ 8 = 7	48 ÷ 8 = 6	8 ÷ 8 = 1
64 ÷ 8 = 8	64 ÷ 8 = 8	56 ÷ 8 = 7
72 ÷ 8 = 9	8 ÷ 8 = 1	16 ÷ 8 = 2
8 ÷ 8 = 1	56 ÷ 8 = 7	64 ÷ 8 = 8

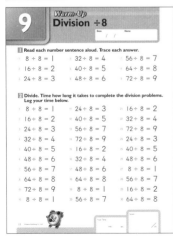

---

10 — Warm-Up: Division ÷9

1 Read each number sentence aloud. Trace each answer.

9 ÷ 9 = 1	36 ÷ 9 = 4	63 ÷ 9 = 7
18 ÷ 9 = 2	45 ÷ 9 = 5	72 ÷ 9 = 8
27 ÷ 9 = 3	54 ÷ 9 = 6	81 ÷ 9 = 9

2 Divide. Time how long it takes to complete the division problems. Log your time below.

9 ÷ 9 = 1	36 ÷ 9 = 4	9 ÷ 9 = 1
18 ÷ 9 = 2	54 ÷ 9 = 6	81 ÷ 9 = 9
27 ÷ 9 = 3	72 ÷ 9 = 8	36 ÷ 9 = 4
36 ÷ 9 = 4	9 ÷ 9 = 1	63 ÷ 9 = 7
45 ÷ 9 = 5	27 ÷ 9 = 3	9 ÷ 9 = 1
54 ÷ 9 = 6	45 ÷ 9 = 5	72 ÷ 9 = 8
63 ÷ 9 = 7	63 ÷ 9 = 7	18 ÷ 9 = 2
72 ÷ 9 = 8	81 ÷ 9 = 9	63 ÷ 9 = 7
81 ÷ 9 = 9	27 ÷ 9 = 3	45 ÷ 9 = 5
18 ÷ 9 = 2	54 ÷ 9 = 6	81 ÷ 9 = 9

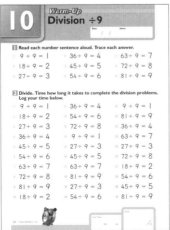

---

11 — Warm-Up: Division ÷1

1 Read each number sentence aloud. Trace each answer.

1 ÷ 1 = 1	4 ÷ 1 = 4	7 ÷ 1 = 7
2 ÷ 1 = 2	5 ÷ 1 = 5	8 ÷ 1 = 8
3 ÷ 1 = 3	6 ÷ 1 = 6	9 ÷ 1 = 9

2 Divide. Time how long it takes to complete the division problems. Log your time below.

1 ÷ 1 = 1	3 ÷ 1 = 3	6 ÷ 1 = 6
2 ÷ 1 = 2	5 ÷ 1 = 5	3 ÷ 1 = 3
3 ÷ 1 = 3	7 ÷ 1 = 7	8 ÷ 1 = 8
4 ÷ 1 = 4	9 ÷ 1 = 9	9 ÷ 1 = 9
5 ÷ 1 = 5	2 ÷ 1 = 2	4 ÷ 1 = 4
6 ÷ 1 = 6	4 ÷ 1 = 4	2 ÷ 1 = 2
7 ÷ 1 = 7	6 ÷ 1 = 6	7 ÷ 1 = 7
8 ÷ 1 = 8	8 ÷ 1 = 8	5 ÷ 1 = 5
9 ÷ 1 = 9	5 ÷ 1 = 5	6 ÷ 1 = 6
1 ÷ 1 = 1	4 ÷ 1 = 4	1 ÷ 1 = 1

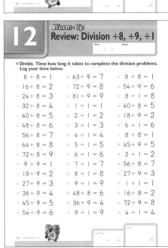

---

12 — Warm-Up: Review: Division ÷8, ÷9, ÷1

● Divide. Time how long it takes to complete the division problems. Log your time below.

8 ÷ 8 = 1	63 ÷ 9 = 7	8 ÷ 8 = 1
16 ÷ 8 = 2	72 ÷ 9 = 8	54 ÷ 9 = 6
24 ÷ 8 = 3	81 ÷ 9 = 9	8 ÷ 1 = 8
32 ÷ 8 = 4	1 ÷ 1 = 1	40 ÷ 8 = 5
40 ÷ 8 = 5	2 ÷ 1 = 2	18 ÷ 9 = 2
48 ÷ 8 = 6	3 ÷ 1 = 3	6 ÷ 1 = 6
56 ÷ 8 = 7	4 ÷ 1 = 4	8 ÷ 8 = 1
64 ÷ 8 = 8	5 ÷ 1 = 5	45 ÷ 9 = 5
72 ÷ 8 = 9	6 ÷ 1 = 6	2 ÷ 1 = 2
18 ÷ 9 = 2	7 ÷ 1 = 7	56 ÷ 8 = 7
27 ÷ 9 = 3	8 ÷ 1 = 8	27 ÷ 9 = 3
36 ÷ 9 = 4	9 ÷ 1 = 9	1 ÷ 1 = 1
45 ÷ 9 = 5	36 ÷ 9 = 4	16 ÷ 8 = 2
54 ÷ 9 = 6	9 ÷ 1 = 9	72 ÷ 8 = 9
		4 ÷ 1 = 4

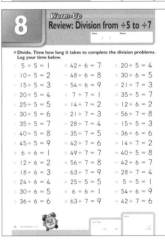

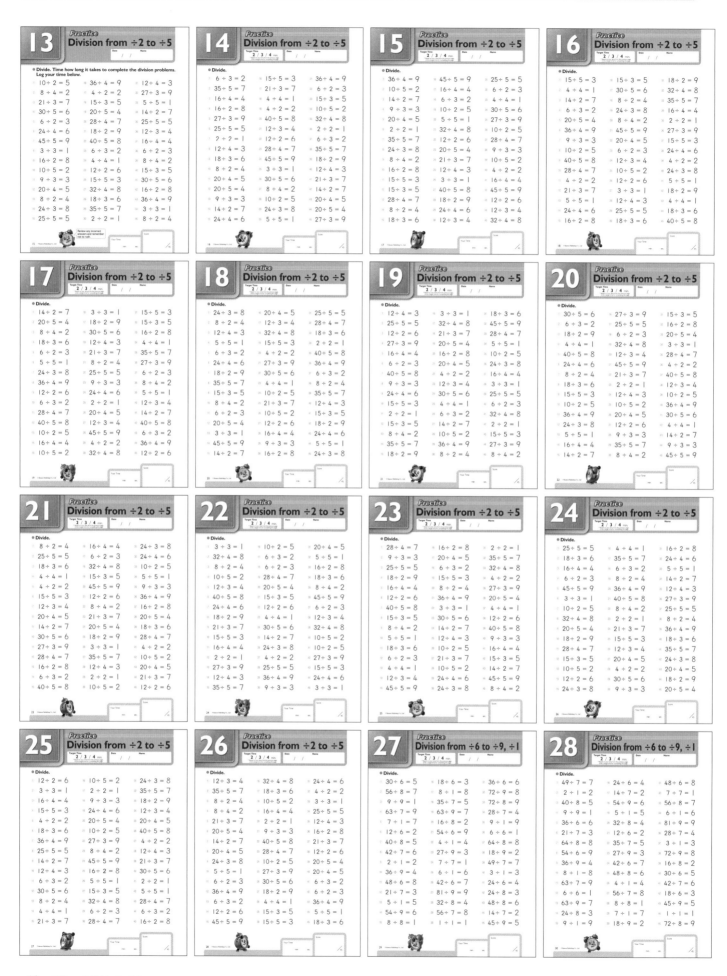

13 Practice — Division from ÷2 to ÷5

Divide. Time how long it takes to complete the division problems. Log your time below.

14 Practice — Division from ÷2 to ÷5

Divide.

15 Practice — Division from ÷2 to ÷5

Divide.

16 Practice — Division from ÷2 to ÷5

Divide.

17 Practice — Division from ÷2 to ÷5

Divide.

18 Practice — Division from ÷2 to ÷5

Divide.

19 Practice — Division from ÷2 to ÷5

Divide.

20 Practice — Division from ÷2 to ÷5

Divide.

21 Practice — Division from ÷2 to ÷5

Divide.

22 Practice — Division from ÷2 to ÷5

Divide.

23 Practice — Division from ÷2 to ÷5

Divide.

24 Practice — Division from ÷2 to ÷5

Divide.

25 Practice — Division from ÷2 to ÷5

Divide.

26 Practice — Division from ÷2 to ÷5

Divide.

27 Practice — Division from ÷6 to ÷9, ÷1

Divide.

28 Practice — Division from ÷6 to ÷9, ÷1

Divide.

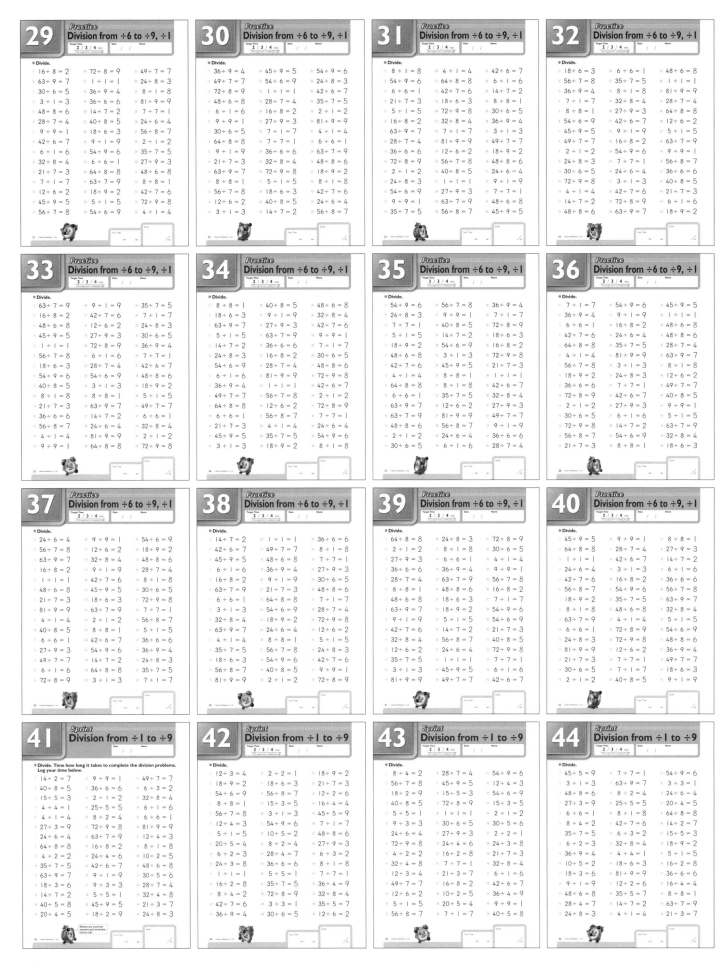

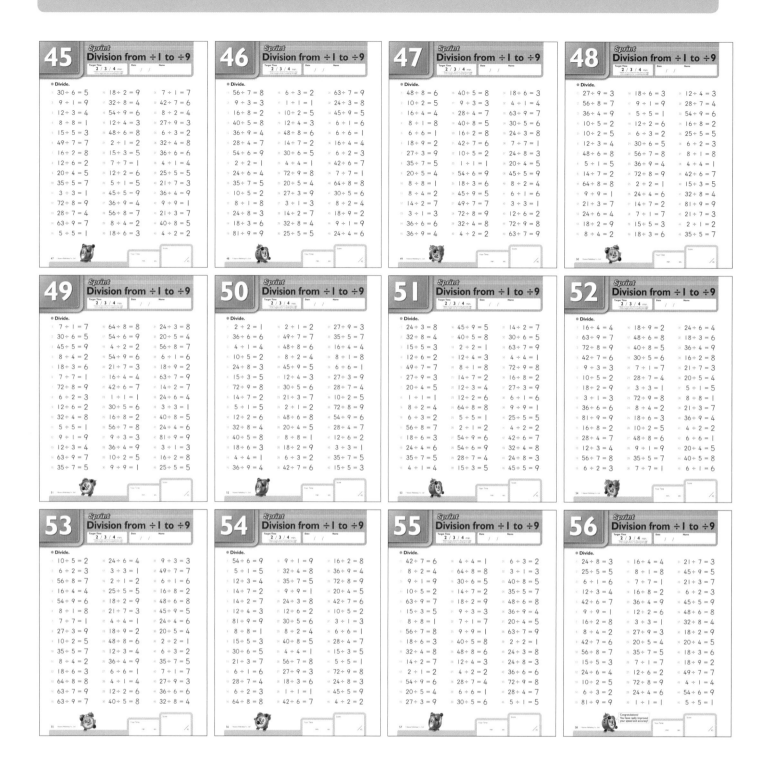

45 Sprint — Division from ÷1 to ÷9
Target Time 2 / 3 / 4 min. · Date / / · Name

● Divide.

30÷6=5	18÷2=9	7÷1=7
9÷1=9	32÷8=4	42÷7=6
12÷3=4	54÷9=6	8÷2=4
8÷8=1	12÷4=3	27÷9=3
15÷5=3	48÷6=8	6÷3=2
49÷7=7	2÷1=2	32÷4=8
16÷2=8	15÷3=5	36÷6=6
12÷6=2	7÷7=1	4÷1=4
20÷5=4	12÷2=6	25÷5=5
35÷5=7	5÷1=5	21÷7=3
3÷3=1	45÷5=9	36÷4=9
72÷9=8	36÷9=4	9÷9=1
28÷7=4	56÷8=7	21÷3=7
63÷9=7	8÷4=2	40÷8=5
5÷5=1	18÷6=3	4÷2=2

46 Sprint — Division from ÷1 to ÷9
Target Time 2 / 3 / 4 min. · Date / / · Name

● Divide.

56÷7=8	6÷3=2	63÷7=9
9÷3=3	1÷1=1	24÷3=8
16÷8=2	10÷2=5	45÷9=5
40÷5=8	12÷4=3	6÷1=6
36÷9=4	48÷8=6	6÷6=1
28÷4=7	14÷7=2	16÷4=4
54÷6=9	30÷6=5	6÷2=3
2÷2=1	4÷4=1	42÷6=7
24÷6=4	72÷9=8	7÷7=1
35÷7=5	20÷5=4	64÷8=8
10÷5=2	27÷9=3	30÷5=6
8÷1=8	3÷1=3	9÷1=9
24÷8=3	14÷2=7	18÷9=2
18÷3=6	32÷8=4	9÷1=9
81÷9=9	25÷5=5	24÷4=6

47 Sprint — Division from ÷1 to ÷9
Target Time 2 / 3 / 4 min. · Date / / · Name

● Divide.

48÷8=6	40÷5=8	18÷6=3
10÷2=5	9÷3=3	4÷1=4
16÷4=4	28÷4=7	63÷9=7
8÷1=8	40÷8=5	30÷5=6
6÷6=1	16÷2=8	24÷3=8
18÷9=2	42÷7=6	7÷7=1
27÷3=9	10÷5=2	24÷8=3
35÷7=5	1÷1=1	20÷4=5
20÷5=4	54÷6=9	45÷5=9
8÷8=1	18÷3=6	8÷2=4
8÷4=2	45÷9=5	6÷1=6
14÷7=2	49÷7=7	3÷3=1
3÷1=3	72÷9=8	12÷6=2
36÷6=6	32÷4=8	72÷9=8
36÷9=4	4÷2=2	63÷7=9

48 Sprint — Division from ÷1 to ÷9
Target Time 2 / 3 / 4 min. · Date / / · Name

● Divide.

27÷9=3	18÷6=3	12÷4=3
56÷8=7	9÷1=9	28÷7=4
36÷4=9	5÷5=1	54÷9=6
10÷5=2	12÷6=2	16÷8=2
10÷2=5	6÷3=2	25÷5=5
12÷3=4	30÷6=5	6÷2=3
48÷6=8	56÷7=8	8÷1=8
5÷1=5	36÷9=4	4÷4=1
14÷7=2	72÷8=9	15÷3=5
64÷8=8	2÷2=1	32÷8=4
9÷9=1	24÷4=6	81÷9=9
24÷6=4	14÷7=2	21÷7=3
18÷2=9	7÷1=7	2÷1=2
8÷4=2	15÷3=5	35÷5=7

49 Sprint — Division from ÷1 to ÷9
Target Time 2 / 3 / 4 min. · Date / / · Name

● Divide.

7÷1=7	64÷8=8	24÷3=8
30÷6=5	54÷6=9	20÷5=4
45÷5=9	4÷2=2	56÷8=7
8÷4=2	54÷9=6	6÷1=6
18÷3=6	21÷7=3	18÷9=2
7÷7=1	16÷4=4	63÷7=9
72÷8=9	42÷6=7	14÷2=7
6÷2=3	1÷1=1	24÷6=4
12÷6=2	30÷5=6	3÷3=1
32÷4=8	16÷8=2	40÷8=5
5÷5=1	56÷7=8	24÷4=6
9÷1=9	9÷3=3	81÷9=9
12÷3=4	36÷4=9	3÷1=3
63÷9=7	10÷2=5	16÷2=8
35÷7=5	9÷9=1	25÷5=5

50 Sprint — Division from ÷1 to ÷9
Target Time 2 / 3 / 4 min. · Date / / · Name

● Divide.

2÷2=1	2÷1=2	27÷9=3
36÷6=6	49÷7=7	35÷5=7
4÷1=4	48÷8=6	16÷4=4
10÷5=2	8÷2=4	8÷1=8
24÷8=3	45÷9=5	6÷6=1
15÷3=5	12÷4=3	27÷3=9
72÷9=8	30÷5=6	28÷7=4
14÷7=2	21÷3=7	10÷2=5
5÷1=5	2÷1=2	72÷8=9
12÷2=6	48÷6=8	54÷9=6
32÷8=4	20÷4=5	12÷6=2
40÷5=8	8÷8=1	3÷3=1
18÷6=3	18÷2=9	35÷7=5
4÷4=1	6÷3=2	15÷5=3
36÷9=4	42÷7=6	

51 Sprint — Division from ÷1 to ÷9
Target Time 2 / 3 / 4 min. · Date / / · Name

● Divide.

24÷3=8	45÷9=5	14÷2=7
32÷8=4	40÷5=8	30÷6=5
15÷5=3	2÷2=1	63÷7=9
12÷6=2	12÷4=3	4÷4=1
49÷7=7	8÷1=8	72÷9=8
27÷9=3	14÷7=2	16÷8=2
20÷4=5	12÷3=4	27÷3=9
1÷1=1	12÷2=6	6÷1=6
8÷2=4	64÷8=8	9÷9=1
6÷3=2	5÷5=1	25÷5=5
56÷8=7	2÷1=2	4÷2=2
18÷6=3	54÷9=6	42÷6=7
24÷4=6	54÷6=9	32÷4=8
35÷7=5	28÷7=4	24÷8=3
4÷1=4	15÷3=5	45÷5=9

52 Sprint — Division from ÷1 to ÷9
Target Time 2 / 3 / 4 min. · Date / / · Name

● Divide.

16÷4=4	18÷9=2	24÷6=4
63÷9=7	48÷6=8	18÷3=6
72÷8=9	40÷8=5	36÷4=9
42÷7=6	30÷5=6	16÷2=8
9÷3=3	7÷1=7	21÷7=3
10÷5=2	28÷7=4	20÷5=4
18÷2=9	3÷3=1	5÷1=5
3÷1=3	72÷9=8	8÷8=1
36÷6=6	8÷4=2	21÷3=7
81÷9=9	18÷6=3	36÷9=4
16÷8=2	10÷2=5	4÷2=2
28÷4=7	48÷8=6	6÷6=1
12÷3=4	9÷1=9	20÷4=5
56÷7=8	35÷5=7	40÷5=8
6÷2=3	7÷7=1	6÷1=6

53 Sprint — Division from ÷1 to ÷9
Target Time 2 / 3 / 4 min. · Date / / · Name

● Divide.

10÷5=2	24÷6=4	9÷3=3
6÷2=3	3÷3=1	49÷7=7
56÷8=7	2÷1=2	6÷1=6
16÷4=4	25÷5=5	16÷8=2
54÷9=6	18÷2=9	48÷6=8
8÷1=8	21÷7=3	45÷9=5
27÷3=9	18÷9=2	24÷4=6
10÷2=5	48÷8=6	20÷5=4
35÷7=5	12÷3=4	2÷2=1
8÷4=2	36÷4=9	35÷7=5
18÷6=3	6÷6=1	7÷1=7
64÷8=8	4÷1=4	27÷9=3
63÷7=9	40÷5=8	36÷6=6
63÷9=7		32÷8=4

54 Sprint — Division from ÷1 to ÷9
Target Time 2 / 3 / 4 min. · Date / / · Name

● Divide.

54÷6=9	9÷1=9	16÷2=8
5÷1=5	32÷4=8	36÷9=4
12÷3=4	35÷7=5	72÷8=9
14÷7=2	9÷9=1	20÷5=4
14÷2=7	24÷3=8	42÷7=6
12÷4=3	12÷6=2	10÷5=2
81÷9=9	30÷5=6	3÷1=3
8÷8=1	8÷2=4	6÷6=1
15÷5=3	40÷8=5	28÷4=7
30÷6=5	4÷4=1	15÷3=5
21÷3=7	56÷7=8	5÷5=1
6÷1=6	27÷9=3	72÷9=8
28÷7=4	18÷3=6	24÷8=3
64÷8=8	1÷1=1	45÷9=5
	42÷6=7	4÷2=2

55 Sprint — Division from ÷1 to ÷9
Target Time 2 / 3 / 4 min. · Date / / · Name

● Divide.

42÷7=6	4÷4=1	6÷3=2
8÷2=4	64÷8=8	3÷1=3
9÷1=9	30÷6=5	40÷8=5
10÷5=2	14÷7=2	35÷5=7
63÷9=7	18÷2=9	48÷6=8
15÷3=5	9÷3=3	36÷9=4
8÷1=8	7÷1=7	20÷4=5
56÷7=8	9÷9=1	63÷7=9
18÷6=3	40÷5=8	2÷2=1
32÷4=8	48÷8=6	24÷3=8
14÷2=7	12÷4=3	24÷8=3
2÷1=2	4÷2=2	36÷6=6
54÷9=6	28÷7=4	72÷9=8
20÷5=4	6÷6=1	28÷4=7
27÷3=9	30÷5=6	5÷1=5

56 Sprint — Division from ÷1 to ÷9
Target Time 2 / 3 / 4 min. · Date / / · Name

● Divide.

24÷8=3	16÷4=4	21÷7=3
25÷5=5	8÷1=8	45÷9=5
6÷1=6	7÷7=1	21÷3=7
12÷3=4	16÷8=2	6÷2=3
42÷6=7	36÷4=9	45÷5=9
9÷9=1	12÷6=2	48÷6=8
8÷4=2	27÷9=3	18÷2=9
42÷7=6	20÷5=4	20÷4=5
15÷5=3	35÷7=5	18÷9=2
24÷6=4	7÷1=7	49÷7=7
10÷2=5	12÷6=2	4÷1=4
6÷3=2	72÷9=8	54÷6=9
81÷9=9	24÷4=6	5÷1=5
	1÷1=1	

Congratulations!
You have really improved your speed and accuracy!

KUM◯N

Certificate of Achievement

is hereby congratulated on completing

Kumon Speed & Accuracy Math Workbook

Division: Dividing Numbers 1 Through 9

Presented on _____ , 20____

_____
Parent or Guardian